Mercedes-Benz G-4

Luftwaffe Field Marshal Hermann Göring's arrival in Danzig in the former Polish Corridor on Sept. 21, 1939, two days after that of the ***Führer***'s triumphal entry, with Gen. Karl Bodenschatz (right rear) behind him. The car is G-4 license plate 1A-100199. (Previously-unpublished photograph by Helmuth Kurth, the Hermann Göring Albums, Library of Congress, Wash., DC.)

Hitler's Chariots

Vol 1

Mercedes-Benz G-4 Cross-Country Touring Car

Blaine Taylor

Schiffer Military History
Atglen, PA

Dedication

To Roger Arend Wychgram, ATVM, Aberdeen, MD/USA, curator of the Mercedes-Benz Roger Wychgram Collection.

Acknowledgments

Herr Wolfgang Rabus of the DaimlerChrysler Archive, Stuttgart, Germany.

Stan Piet (Photographic Consultant) of Bel Air, MD/USA. Piet assisted the author by copying literally thousands of photographs held in various U.S. archives.

Ralph Louis Engelstad (1930-2002), owner of the Imperial Palace Hotel and Casino, for allowing me access to his collection of Mercedes-Benz G-4 cars. I would also like to thank the Collection Administrator, Richie Clyne.

Mrs. Erika Burke for her tireless efforts translating many German language documents.

Roger Wychgram of ATVM, Aberdeen, MD, for all of his prior help in developing this series of Mercedes works.

Book Design by Ian Robertson.

Library of Congress Control Number: 2008943091

Printed in China.
ISBN: 978-0-7643-3236-4

We are interested in hearing from authors with book ideas on related topics.

Published by Schiffer Publishing Ltd.
4880 Lower Valley Road
Atglen, PA 19310
Phone: (610) 593-1777
FAX: (610) 593-2002
E-mail: Info@schifferbooks.com.
Visit our web site at: www.schifferbooks.com
Please write for a free catalog.
This book may be purchased from the publisher.
Please include $5.00 postage.
Try your bookstore first.

In Europe, Schiffer books are distributed by:
Bushwood Books
6 Marksbury Avenue
Kew Gardens
Surrey TW9 4JF, England
Phone: 44 (0) 20 8392-8585
FAX: 44 (0) 20 8392-9876
E-mail: Info@bushwoodbooks.co.uk.
Visit our website at: www.bushwoodbooks.co.uk

Contents

On March 1, 1940, *Luftwaffe* Field Marshal Hermann Göring's G-4 license plate 1A-100199 is seen at West Langendiebach Airport during the Western Front campaign, with all bulletproof windows rolled up and lamp covers on. The field marshal sits next to the *SS* chauffeur in front, while Air Force Gen. Hugo Sperrle glares at the camera from the right mid-car jump seat, with three other *Luftwaffe* officers in the rear seat behind. (Previously-unpublished photograph by Helmuth Kurth, the Hermann Göring Albums, Library of Congress, Wash., DC.)

Introduction
The Wartime Mercedes-Benz G-4 Cross-Country Touring Cars

In the main, Nazi German *Führer* (Leader) Adolf Hitler set aside his former 770K Grosser Mercedes-Benz parade cars for his personal usage during most of the Second World War in favor of the more rugged Daimler G-4 model.

As I noted in my 1999 book *Mercedes-Benz Parade and Staff Cars of the Third Reich*:

> "The *Führer* used his cars throughout the wartime years, starting in Poland where he toured the battlefields, entering Danzig in triumph and Warsaw in silence, all in his G-4 cross-country vehicles.
>
> "There is no evidence to indicate that he ever visited conquered Norway, Denmark or the Netherlands in any mode of transportation, but he did travel in Belgium and France in the G-4s, and made a single, much-publicized trip to fallen Paris on June 23, 1940 in the G-4 car.
>
> "He made no trips to vanquished Greece or Yugoslavia, but several to the German-occupied Soviet Union, first in August 1941 with Mussolini to the Ukraine, and later to visit Army Field Marshals Fedor von Bock and Gerd von Rundstedt in 1942, and Erich von Manstein in 1943.
>
> "In all cases, he used the G-4, and also his own cars, and ferried them out often hundreds of miles for a drive of perhaps a few hundred yards. He didn't trust his Army generals with his life in their cars. On at least one occasion, there was an Army plot to arrest him in a car during one of these visits, but the plot died.
>
> "So far as is known, there was never any plot—either Allied or German—to assassinate Hitler in his cars as in the attack on Heydrich."

In fact, I was wrong when I wrote those words, but I didn't know it. Indeed, the year before (1998) Her Majesty's Royal Public Record Office published a secret wartime report entitled *Operation Foxley: The British Plan to Kill Hitler* that did feature an assault on him in one of his cars, but this information was not yet available to me in the United States. I hereby rectify that error:

> "At his primary Eastern Front *Führerhauptquartier* (FHQ—Leader Headquarters) at Rastenburg in East Prussia, Wolfsschanze (Wolf's Lair), both the Grosser Mercedes and the G-4s were used...Besides the Grossers, G-4s, and the Horch car in the *Führer's* garage fleets during the war, there was perhaps yet another vehicle...the 1938-42 Mercedes-Benz V-12, Type 600."

As noted by author Peter Hoffmann in his excellent 1979 work *Hitler's Personal Security*:

> "Touring cars of Type 520G4W31 and 131 were manufactured from 1934-39, and delivered up until 1940. They were built with three axles, and could be used for cross-country travel as well as for parades and other occasions when speed was not required. They had 5-liter (W31) and 5.252-liter (W131) eight-cylinder engines delivering 98 hp (W131) respectively, but according to (SS Col. chauffeur Erich) Kempka, Hitler used only the large 7.7 liter cars which could go up to 75mph
>
> "These cars were used preferably on public and semi-public occasions, and on visits to theaters of war. They had 30mm windshields, the roll-up windows on both sides of the front seats were 20mm thick, and the rear side-windows were 30mm thick. The back of the rear seats were reinforced with 8mm steel plate and came up as high as the tops of the passengers' heads. With 8mm steel doors and an equally reinforced enclosure for the driver's leg room and floor plates, this car was moderately bulletproof against the handguns and rifles then in use.
>
> "The bulletproof tires were taken off, however, because they caused heavy vibration. Ordinary tires with extremely low air pressure had to be used for the sake of Hitler's oversensitive stomach. Since his cars were only canvas-top tourers, however, moderately protected only at their sides, shots and grenades could be dropped in from above, and Hitler liked standing up in his car, thus raising chest and head well above the light armor. He declared later that it was foolish for others to do this after Heydrich was assassinated in Prague in May 1942.
>
> "'Since it is the opportunity which makes not only the thief but also the assassin, such heroic gestures as driving in an open unarmored vehicle...are just damned stupidity, which serves the country not one damned whit!' It is significant to note, too, that after the Heydrich assassination, Hitler himself almost never did this again."

As I again noted in 1999:

> "When war with Poland broke out in September 1939, Hitler as Supreme Commander went to inspect his newly-conquered foreign territory: 'All cars were open Mercedes, still in glossy beige with black mudguards,' writes Peter Hoffmann, 'but with license plates and other insignia covered.' By the time of the French campaign, the (G-4) cars were painted dull olive-gray. 'Two groups were formed... Hitler's group was preceded by a squad of five soldiers on motorcycles and by two armed reconnaissance vehicles, and five more motorcycle soldiers brought up the rear.'"

This, then, was the famous wartime *Führerkolonne* (Leader Column) that was seen by German soldiers speeding across first the plains of Poland, and later through Northwestern Europe in 1940.

One who had a personal experience with the *Führer* Column was a young Jewish-German Army officer named Alexander Stahlberg, author of the superb 1990 memoir *Bounden Duty*, who recalled therein this incident in Poland in September 1939:

> "We were still advancing, without having fired a shot (when) an order came over the radio: 'Turn right off the road, stop, wait.' We knew that meant that a force urgently needed further forward was to be let through ahead of us.
>
> "Sure enough, an armored reconnaissance car came up behind us, traveling at high speed...From the turret protruded the figure of a general, unrecognizable in his dust-goggles, but round his neck we spotted the highest Prussian military order, Pour le Merite. As the dust cloud moved away, we could hear more vehicles approaching and a large, shapeless open Mercedes appeared, traveling at the same high speed—a model we had not seen before, a three-axle, cross-country vehicle. In the front passenger seat sat Hitler, in gray uniform, which was also new to us.
>
> "A few more vehicles followed close behind, at breakneck speed, considering the dust cloud from the first vehicle. 'That, too,' remarked Yorck drily, 'like Lutzow's witch hunt.' I wanted to know who the general in the leading scout car had been. We would find out at once, Yorck told me, going over to the radio car behind us. He returned soon afterwards with the news that it was a general called Rommel."

What follows is the interesting saga of those famed *Führerkolonne* G-4 cross-country cars, of which but 57 were ever made, and some of automotive history's most interesting and most photographed vehicles.

Blaine Taylor
Berkshires at Town Center
Towson, MD

A joyous Hitler surrounded by happy people during his entry into Karlovy Vary/Karlsbad on Oct. 4, 1938. At left center is his NSKK/Nazi Party Motor Corps aide Albert Bormann, younger brother of Martin Bormann. (HHA.)

Feb. 29, 1940: A previously-unpublished photo of *Luftwaffe* Field Marshal Hermann Göring at the Trier, Germany, train station in G-4 license plate IA 100199, a Berlin registry vehicle. Göring sits up front next to his *SS* chauffeur. The lamp covers are on and the engine radiator cover is rolled up. (HGA.)

1

Dr. Ferdinand Porsche and the G-4 Model

Dr. Ferdinand Porsche the Elder (1875-1951) had an explosive personality. Once, during a Daimler-Benz Board of Directors meeting, he threw a cigarette lighter at a member who'd angered him. Another time, he took off his trademark Homburg hat during a heated argument and reportedly jumped up and down on it in fury. When Board Chairman Dr. Wilhelm Kissel challenged him one morning to "cold start" his Mercedes Stuttgart models after their being left out one freezing night and he couldn't, Dr. Porsche stormed off in a huff, resigned on Dec. 31, 1928, and founded his own design firm. He would not return to Daimler-Benz for a full decade.

His relations with Nazi Germany's *Führer* and Reich Chancellor Adolf Hitler were much more amiable, however. They first met at the 1924 Solitude road race, when Dr. Porsche was already the most famous car designer in Europe, and the former First World War *gefreiter (*American Army private first class) was but an obscure Bavarian politician on the make.

Nine years later, however, the situation had changed, and Hitler was the new Head of Government, who invited the eminent engineer to the Reich Chancellery in Berlin for a chat about a project dear to both their hearts: the building of a new People's Car, or Volkswagen. The *Führer* cooed, "I have arranged for sausages and beer. Okay?"

After Hitler opened his first Berlin International Automobile and Motorcycle Exhibition as Reich Chancellor on Feb. 11, 1933, Dr. Porsche secured another meeting with Chancellor Hitler to discuss the building of a new race car by Auto-Union, Mercedes' greatest rival at the time. By now, the *Führer* was already famed for not changing his mind once he'd made a decision, but he made a rare exception in this case and split the money allocated for a single race car to be built by Daimler in half to include one designed by Porsche for Auto-Union as well. It was a signal victory for the fiery-tempered automotive genius.

According to his son, co-worker, and later successor in the family's design firm, Dr. Ferry Porsche:

> "At most, a half-dozen men in all of Germany dared to speak their minds openly before Hitler, and my father was one of them...The situation, in fact, was in some respects as though my father were also Hitler's father...My father was able to influence Hitler's opinion, though of course only in technical matters."

In time, not only would Dr. Porsche build still-famous supercharged automobiles for Daimler-Benz and racers for Auto-Union, but also the Volkswagen that sparked the "West German economic miracle" of the 1950s after his death, as well as the wartime King Tiger, Panther, Ferdinand, and *Maus* (Mouse) tanks for the armored panzer divisions of the Third Reich.

Dr. Porsche also had a significant impact on the development of the G-4 cross-country touring car so favored by Hitler that they appear in many prewar and wartime newsreels as his car of choice when entering newly fallen lands and their capitals.

By the time his future *Führer* was born in 1889, Ferdinand Porsche was already 14 years old and working in his father's tinsmith shop at Maffersdorf, Bohemia, where he was born on Sept. 8, 1875, a subject—like Hitler later—of the Dual Monarchy of the Habsburg Dynasty, the Austro-Hungarian Empire ruled by Kaiser (Emperor) Franz Josef.

Not until 1934 did Dr. Porsche become a German citizen, when it was forced upon him by order of Nazi Propaganda Minister Dr. Josef Göbbels.

By age 19 in 1894, Porsche had built his own electric generator system that he installed in his father's home. Porsche Sr. wanted his son to follow in the family tinsmith business, but young Ferdinand's own interests were in the fields of electricity and engineering. Initially trained as a plumber, through at-home self-study he progressed to becoming an engineer, and got a job with the Lohner Automobile Factory in Vienna. In 1900, Porsche designed and built a car that would still be considered unique even by today's standards, as it had a power train with twin electric *motors* in the *front* wheels! Its introduction at the 1900 Paris Universal Exposition gained him global fame for the first time.

Six years later, Porsche joined the Austro-Daimler Company, and within 10 years was its General Director. The firm built under his stewardship internal combustion engines that garnered both it and the engineer more international acclaim.

During the First World War, Porsche designed 80-ton gun carriages for the Imperial Austrian Army, working with a 20-year-old officer named Alfred Neubauer, who would become a race car driver, Mercedes racing team manager, and both lifelong Porsche rival and co-worker after the war.

Following the defeat of the Central Powers, Porsche found himself in 1923 at the Daimler Motor Company plant at Stuttgart, Germany. Ironically, he was fated to succeed the founder's son, Paul Daimler, twice as Technical Director: first in 1906 at the Austro-Daimler Works, and then again in 1923 at the Unterturkheim, Germany, plant.

Porsche picked up where Paul Daimler had left off in the development of a supercharged car for Daimler that became the Mercedes-Benz after the two companies merged on June 28, 1926, building all the elephant blower "Kompressor" supercharged "S" cars of the Twenties and Thirties that were so beloved by all the top Nazi leaders, beginning in 1927.

The S series included the S (Sports), SS (Super Sport), SSK (Super Sport Short), and SSKL. These cars went on to win race after race, making Mercedes one of the most famous cars in the world, and sending sales charts ever upwards until the outbreak of the Second World War in 1939.

His son and heir Ferry Porsche was born on Sept. 19, 1909, at the Villa Porsche at Wiener Neustadt (Vienna New Town), an industrial suburb of the Austrian Imperial capital city. Even as a little boy, Ferry worked with his father on all automotive projects, and went on to reestablish the design firm after World War II while his father was a political prisoner of the French. In 1976, Ferry published his excellent memoirs *We at Porsche*.

Accounts differ as to when Ferdinand Porsche was awarded the title of doctor. Some say he received it as the result of one of his cars having won the 1922 Italian *Targa Florio* race in Sicily, while writer Walter Henry Nelson gives this account in his VW history *Small Wonder*:

> "In 1917, Porsche received an honorary doctorate in engineering from Vienna Technical University. Herr Doktor Porsche…had achieved academic acceptance, and the proud title never left his calling cards."

Ferry graduated from VTU as well with a degree in engineering, and thus there were *two* Drs. Porsche.

By 1929, father and son were building cars in the garage of the family home at Feuerbacherweg, in Stuttgart, and Ferry officially joined the Porsche Design Firm factory workshops at Zuffenhausen in 1933. The year before, a Soviet delegation had come to meet Porsche the Elder, inviting him to tour the automotive facilities of the USSR at the personal behest of dictator Josef Stalin.

He left for Russia on July 20, 1932, and went everywhere he wanted to, seeing everything he asked concerning the Soviet car industry, which impressed him. The tour included the Volga River-sited city of Stalingrad. Stalin offered him a villa for himself, his family, and staff in the Crimea, complete with a blank check arrangement to design and build whatever he wanted to. Once back in the Reich, however, Dr. Porsche declined, mainly because he felt that the language translation difficulties inherent in imparting technical data to his Russian assistants would be insurmountable.

Had he become a Red Army POW in 1945 instead of being captured by the French, Dr. Porsche might well have been offered the same option again—or been shot by an angry Stalin for his wartime work for Hitler, all of it used against the USSR.

As it was, on Sept. 6, 1938, Dr. Porsche—along with aircraft designers Ernst Heinkel and Willi Messerschmitt, and Autobahn (highway) engineer Fritz Todt (doctors all)—was awarded the German National Prize for Art and Science, the Nazi counterpart to the Nobel Peace Prize. Presented by Hitler personally at the Nazi Party Congress at Nurnberg, the award included a medal and a financial gift of 25,000 Reichsmarks. Present at the event were most of the top Nazi leadership cadre, including Field Marshal Hermann Göring, under whose economic Four Year Plan the Porsches would work closely for the next eight years.

With the war's coming in September 1939, Hitler decreed a virtual end to the building of German commercial passenger cars, and international racing was halted, too. Thus, the German automotive industry and the Porsche Design Firm became handmaidens to the ever-expanding Reich war effort instead.

In December 1941, at the *Führer*'s order, Dr. Porsche the Elder was flown to the German-occupied area of the USSR by Hitler's personal pilot, Col. Hans Baur, in his capacity as Head of the Panzer (Armored) Commission to inspect and evaluate captured Red Army T-34 tanks, the best such medium-sized vehicles built by either side in the war.

When Ferry asked for his father's conclusions, the latter answered:

> "I am more convinced than ever that success lies in the direction of weapons and war materiel made as simply as possible. We should turn away from this mania to produce always more complex and sophisticated equipment."

This was also the view of the new Reich Minister for Armaments and War Production, Hitler's former architect, Albert Speer, who took over from the dead Dr. Todt on Feb. 8, 1942, after the latter had been killed in a still-mysterious air crash.

Dr. Porsche the Elder and Speer often found themselves at loggerheads, since both were ambitious, determined, and headstrong men, but out of their successful wartime collaboration nonetheless sprang a quartet of famous tanks: the PzKpfw Tiger, the Ferdinand, the PzKpfw Panther, and the *Maus*, the biggest armored vehicle built by either side in the war.

Hitler had long been calling for the replacement of the lighter German tanks of the earlier war years with the heavier models that came on-line by late 1943 on all fighting fronts, and particularly for the development of the 75mm, long-barreled gun with which they were equipped as their main armament.

Dr. Porsche was in full agreement, and the Type 101 Tiger tank was soon undergoing field runs at the Boblingen Panzer Testing Ground outside Stuttgart.

There were 1,350 Tiger I tanks built, followed by 500 Tiger II models called the King Tiger, for a total of 1,850 tanks in all.

German panzers in the 1944 Normandy campaign were superior in every way to those of the Allies, especially the M-4 medium Sherman tank that was used by the Americans, British, and Canadians.

There was a cover-up alleged by Members of Parliament in London who charged that Allied soldiers were fighting against heavier enemy armor plate, as well as guns with more range and power—and that was so.

According to D-Day historian author Max Hastings in his superb 1984 book *Overlord*:

"The Panzer VI—or Tiger—was the most feared German tank in Normandy, almost impenetrable by frontal Allied tank gun fire, and packing a devastating punch with its 88mm KwK 36 gun.

"Muzzle velocity in all guns is chiefly a function of barrel length, and Allied troops were always shocked by their first encounters with the Tiger's gun, 'as long as a telegraph pole,' as so many men reported. Its 20-pound shell could penetrate 120mm of armor at 100 yards, 112mm at 500 yards, 102mm at 1,000 yards.

"The Tiger itself carried 100mm of frontal armor, 80mm of side armor, weighed 54 tons, and had a maximum speed of 23 mph...Its principal shortcomings were clumsiness of movement and lack of mechanical reliability."

A major proponent of longer gun barrels was none other than Adolf Hitler himself, correctly, as it developed.

Next came the Ferdinand in 1942. It weighed 60 tons, had a 315 horsepower engine, and could travel at 21 mph. Its 12.5-foot-long barrel and 18.5 cm gun gave its shells a muzzle velocity of 3,280 feet per second, and a range of 8.25 miles. The shells became known within the German Armored Corps as "Panzer grenades." Then came the Panther. According to Hastings in *Overlord*:

"The Panzer MkV...was the outstanding German tank of the campaign in Northwest Europe, less heavily-gunned but more mobile and reliable than the Tiger. One of the two tank regiments in every German armored division was equipped with the Panther, which weighed 45 tons, could move at 34 mph, and carried 100mm of frontal armor, and 45mm of side armor.

"Its 75mm KwK 43 gun had a muzzle velocity of 3,060 fps, and its 14-pound shell could penetrate 138mm of armor at 100 yards, 128mm at 500 yards, 118mm at 1,000 yards. Its only serious weaknesses against the Sherman were indifferent periscope optics and slow turret traverse."

Added *The Second World War in Color*:

"Designed in response to the Soviet T34, the German Panzer (PzKpwv) tank entered service in the spring of 1943 and proved a remarkable success despite some teething troubles. With a weight of 45 tons (45,000kg), it had frontal armor plating three-four inches 80-100mm) thick.

"It possessed a fine 75mm gun with a high initial rate of fire. Its 700 horsepower Maybach engine permitted a speed of 28 mph (45km/h) over a range of 125 miles (200 km). More than 5,500 of these machines left the MAN factories, and the Panther was engaged in every theater of operations."

The Royal Tiger, or Tiger II, weighed 68 ½ tons, had a crew of five, and a cruising range of 106 miles. For armament, the Royal Tiger boasted a 88mm KwK 43/L71 gun with 78 rounds, and a pair of 7.92mm machine guns with 5,850 rounds. It traveled at 26 mph on roads and 13 cross-country. It had 100mm armor on its lower frontage and turret, 150mm on the upper front, 80mm on the sides, and 40mm on top.

On Hitler's 53rd birthday (Apr. 20, 1942) Minister Speer presented him with a pair of these tanks, "The first production Tigers designed by Professor Porsche, who was awarded a high decoration for his efforts," according to Dutch author Dan van der Vat in *The Good Nazi: The Life and Lies of Albert Speer*.

Added Speer in his 1970-published *Memoirs: Inside the Third Reich*:

"We decided to develop a new 30-ton tank whose very name, Panther, was to signify greater agility. Though light in weight, it could develop superior speed, but in the course of a year, Hitler once again insisted on clapping so much armor on it, as well as larger guns, that it ultimately reached 48 tons, the original weight of the Tiger. In order to compensate for this strange transformation of a swift Panther into a slow Tiger, we made still another effort to produce a series of small, light, quick-moving tanks."

Then there came the *Maus*, or Mouse, tank, which weighed 180 tons. Hitler first saw a full-scale wooden model of this monster tank at *Führer* Headquarters in East Prussia in May 1943. He was ecstatic over the model, even though only a few could be built at a time, and would consume materials that could produce six or seven Tiger tank models.

They could only be built by the autumn of 1944 on, would get but 12 mph, and have "insoluble" supply and spare parts problems, according to Speer, who opposed it, as did the peppery Inspector-General of Panzer Forces, Col. Gen. Heinz Guderian. Speer's own deputy, Karl Otto Saur—who secretly coveted his boss' post for himself—egged Hitler on.

Of the Type 205 *Maus*, Hitler exclaimed to Porsche the Elder, "If I had a hundred of these, I could turn back the Russians!" but by the time the war ended, Nazi Germany had built only four *Maus* prototypes—none of which ever saw action. The Panzer VII, as it was known, was massively armored and carried a 122mm main gun. There were only two Type 205 Mouse tanks manufactured.

According to Tim Kidwell of the U.S. Army Ordnance Museum at Aberdeen, MD/USA Proving Ground on July 13, 2001, "One is in Australia and the other in Russia, as far as we know. The rumor that one is here is not so."

Engineer Joseph Kales of Porsche designed the 44.5-liter engine built by Daimler-Benz. Its output was 1,080 bhp at 2,300 rpm, giving a maximum speed of 12.4 mph. It was 33 feet long and 12 feet wide. Dr. Porsche designed an 88-foot-long railway carriage with 14 axles to transport it. Speer also stated:

"By way of pleasing and reassuring Hitler, Porsche...undertook to design a super heavy tank which weighed over a hundred tons, and hence could only be built in small numbers, one by one.

"For security purposes, this new monster was assigned the codename *Mouse*. In any case, Porsche had personally taken over Hitler's bias for super heaviness and would occasionally bring the *Führer* reports about parallel developments on the part of the enemy."

On January 28, 1947, Speer noted in his secret Spandau prison diary:

"I recall a characteristic episode that took place in May 1943 in the East Prussian headquarters…Hitler was being shown a full-size wooden model of a 180-ton tank that he himself had insisted on.

"Nobody in the tank forces displayed any interest in the production of these monsters, for each of them would have tied up the productive capacity needed to build six or seven Tiger tanks and in addition would present insoluble supply and spare parts problems."

Ironically, the latter were also two of the *Führer*'s own pet peeves. Continued Speer:

"The thing would be much too heavy, much too slow (around 12 miles an hour), and moreover could only be built from the autumn of 1944 on. We—that is, Professor Porsche, Gen. Guderian, Chief of Staff Zeitzler, and I—had agreed before the beginning of the inspection to express our skepticism at least by extreme reserve.

"In keeping with our arrangement, Porsche, when asked by Hitler what he thought of the vehicle, replied tersely in a noncommittal tone: 'Of course, mein *Führer*, we can build such tanks.' The rest of us stood silently in a circle.

"Otto Saur—observing Hitler's disappointment—began to rant enthusiastically about the chances for the monster and its importance in the development of military technology. Within a few minutes, he and Hitler were launched on one of those euphoric raise-the-ante dialogues such as I had had occasionally with Hitler when we discussed future architectural projects.

"Unconfirmed reports on the building of super heavy Russian tanks whipped them up further, until the two—throwing all technical inhibitions to the wind—arrived at the overpowering battle strength of a tank weighing 1,500 tons, which would be transported in sections on railroad cars and put together just before being committed to battle.

"At our request, a much decorated tank colonel had been brought from the front. He finally managed to say that a single hand grenade or an incendiary charge exploded anywhere near the ventilator opening could set fire to the oil vapors of these vehicles.

"Hitler, irritated by the disturbing remark, replied, 'Then we'll equip these tanks with machine guns that can be guided automatically in all directions from inside.' Turning to the tank colonel, he added in a lecturing tone, 'After all, I can say for myself in all modesty that I am no amateur in this field. It was I who rearmed Germany.'

"Of course Hitler knew that the 1,500-ton tank was a monstrosity, but ultimately he was grateful to Saur for giving him such shots in the arm from time to time. In the Testament he drew up shortly before his death, he dismissed me as Minister of Armaments and appointed Saur my successor."

According to noted automobile writer John Bentley—co-author with Dr. Ferry Porsche of *We at Porsche*—in 1943:

"The decision to build the gigantic Type 205 Maus tank gave rise to an immediate problem: that of transporting it. The only way this monster could be moved any distance would be by rail, since any ordinary bridge would collapse under its weight.

"Germany had at the time no railroad car capable of carrying a tank 33 feet long and 12 feet wide. Professor Porsche therefore designed a flat-bed car more than 88 feet long, equipped with 14 axles."

Added Bob Carruthers:

"When the war ended, Germany was still developing the super heavy Panzer VII, a huge metal monster, weighing over 100 tons, massively armored and sporting a huge 122mm main gun…The Maus was never to see action, and only four prototypes were ever built, but it seemed that the crazed minds of the Third Reich would never give up the quest to be the best and the biggest, whatever the cost, but as the humble T34 had proved, in matters of evolution, quantity matters as much as quality."

Thus, with the *Maus* on the extreme end of the size spectrum as per being large—and the VW Beetle on the other with the small—Dr. Porsche had gone from the ridiculous to the sublime within the bare time frame of but two decades!

The war ended on May 8, 1945, with Porsche the Elder a French hostage for the next five years, mainly to force him to design a version of the VW for France, which he refused to do. He was released at last in 1950, and saw the new Porsche 356 #1 designed by Ferry for the reborn firm. Dr. Ferdinand Porsche the Elder died at Stuttgart at age 75 on January 30, 1951, ironically the 17th anniversary of Hitler's appointment as Chancellor in 1933.

This then was the mastermind behind one of Hitler's most famous cars, the Mercedes-Benz G-4 model, of which but 57 in all engine versions were ever produced, most of them still existing worldwide in various collections.

The Model W 31 G-4 cross-country touring car had a four-stroke Otto internal combustion principle engine with eight in-line cylinders. Its configuration was front, longitudinal, and vertical, and it had an 88 by 108 mm bore by stroke. Its M24 engine had a total displacement of 5252 cc, a compression ratio of 5.6, nine crankshaft bearings, and a rated output of 115 horsepower at 3400 rpm.

The G-4's rated torque was 29 mkg at 1400 rpm, and its number of valves was one intake and one overhead exhaust, with a single lateral camshaft valve operation. Its camshaft drive was by spur gears, its fuel system consisted of one double carburetor Solex at 40 MMDVS, and a cooling system of 10 1 oil pressure circulation lubrication.

The G-4's electrical system consisted of 12 V, its battery was 105 Ah, its generator 130 W, and its electrical starter was 1.8 hp. The fuel tank capacity was 90 1, partly also 140 1.

According to Gerhard Heidbrink of DaimlerChrysler AG's Mercedes Car Group's Brand Communications' Product History & Archives to this author of Nov. 20, 2006:

"It is our policy for quite some years now not to publish data on individual cars of our production program—i.e., identification numbers, delivery dates, and customer data.

"Apart from the protection of personal (customer) data, a further reason is to avoid fraudulent manipulations of vehicles and their individual history, based on such pieces of information.

"However, due to the fact that VIN series and yearly production of the G-4 have already been published in the specialist literature, please find...a file with this data...License plate numbers have never been documented in our archives, and we do not know a source where to find them."

On December 13, 2007, Herr Heidbrink further informed me that:

"VIN means Vehicle Identification Number, i.e. chassis number. Thus, the VIN list sent....shows the VINs of the G-4 vehicles," and they follow:

The following G-4s were produced, year-by-year:

1934	6 units
1935	4 units
1936	1 unit
1937	4 units
1938	12 units
1939	30 units
Total	**57 units**
	G-4 VINs
1934	105181-105186
1935	117757-117760
1936	142176
1937	189461-18464
1938-39	406522-406530, 421981-42183
1939-40	440864-440888, 44506-44510

Two giants of the German automotive industry, Reich Chancellor Adolf Hitler and Dr. Ferdinand Porsche (12th and 15th from left, respectively), meet sometime during 1942 or 1943 with some of the latter's mechanical staff within the Third Reich during wartime. On August 20, 1942, the Nazi *Führer* stated in his famed "table talk" at *Führer* Headquarters (FHQ), "Adolf Muller taught me once to drive a car," but no known photographs have ever surfaced showing *Herr* Hitler doing just that! (Photo by Walter Frentz.)

At the Rugenwalde in Pomerania on March 1, 1943, at a demonstration of a giant railroad gun are seen, from left to right, Col. Gen. Alfred Jodl (in right profile), Dr. Ferdinand Porsche, Panzer/Armor Inspector General Gen. Heinz Guderian, Hitler, Field Marshal Wilhelm Keitel, Armaments Ministry official Dr. Karl Otto Saur (Speer's deputy), and an unknown German Army general at far right. The disastrous German 6th Army surrender to the Red Army at Stalingrad, for which the *Führer* took full responsibility before his field marshals and generals, had only just occurred. A turning point of the Second World War was at hand. (Photo by Walter Frentz.)

A splendid cutaway schematic of the chassis of a G-4 cross-country car showing, from left to right, radiator grill, front axle, engine and compressor supercharger valves, steering wheel, transmission, double-wheeled rear axles, fuel tank, and gas cap. (Photo from the Roger Wychgram Collection, Aberdeen, MD/USA.)

Rear seating section armor plating revealed. (Photo from the Mercedes-Benz Albums, Library of Congress, Wash., DC.)

Left and following: In these previously-unpublished photographs from the Hermann Göring Albums, the commander-in-chief of the *Luftwaffe* (center) inspects his new G-4 in 1938, license plate IIA-1316, of Münich registry in Bavaria. Göring wears a Reich Hunting Master kit, complete with feathered cap. According to Hitler's Armaments Minister Dr. Albert Speer, on Jan. 4, 1943, *Reichsführer/National Administrator SS* "Himmler asked me to abolish direction indicators and large headlights on automotive vehicles. The indicators, he said, were hardly necessary, considering the small amount of traffic, and the headlights were not used anyway because of the (wartime night) blackout regulations." (Library of Congress, Washington, DC.)

A Mercedes-Benz G-4 bearing the license plate "SS-41." The vehicle is being driven into the Gleiwitz Daimler plant just before the war for servicing. The special runic license plates were brought in for members of the *SS* organization. The initial G-1 cross-country open tourer was developed between 1926-28. By 1934, the much-improved G-4 underwent initial road testing. Hitler was extremely impressed with the concept of this vehicle, and purchased one of the first built. Only 57 of the incredible G-4s were built. (Mercedes-Benz Albums, LC, Wash., DC.)

Of the 57 G-4s manufactured by Daimler-Benz, until recently it was thought that only three survived: one in the former Soviet Union, another in Czechoslovakia, and a third in France, as seen here in restored condition, complete with German Army Maltese crosses. The license plate is 1A-67510, of Berlin registry. The car's gearbox was a ZF Aphon Type G-35 transmission with four forward gears and a reverse, plus Daimler- Benz auxiliary transmission. The gear ratios were: I=4.11:1; II=2.21:1; III=1.49:1; IV=1:1; R=5.3:1; and auxiliary transmission I=1:1 and II=3.06:1. The car had a dry, single-plate clutch and a box section chassis frame with a wheelbase of 4050mm. The car's weight when empty was 3500kg with Ate-Lockwood mechanical-hydraulic oil-pressure system footbrakes. (U.S. National Archives, College Park, MD/USA.)

A Mercedes-Benz Type G-4 1934 bzw, as seen in 1936. Stated author Jan Melin, "Most of the G-4s stayed in Germany, but a few were sent abroad. One was sent to Spain in 1939, as a gift to Gen. (Francisco) Franco. The G-4s were not equipped with superchargers...but...they have a certain kinship with the supercharged (770K) cars, insofar as they had 8-cylinder engines, based on the M24 engine." The car's displacement was 501cc with a 74kW engine of 100 hp at 3400rpm. Its compression ratio was 5.6:1 with a bore x stroke of 86 x 108mm and a side bottom camshaft valve gear. (MB Albums, LC, Wash., DC.)

A typical prewar black G-4 outside the Sindelfingen Daimler-Benz main administration building. During wartime, they would be painted *Wehrmacht* gray for the *Führer's* famed "Gray Column." This is a 1934 model photographed two years later. (MB Albums, LC, Wash., DC.)

A trio of views of G-4s painted in *Wehrmacht* gray, and as used by Hitler in his prewar entrances into annexed Austria and the former Czech Sudetenland, and during wartime into Belgium, France, and the conquered Ukraine in the former USSR. (MB Albums, LC, Wash., DC.)

A pair of Air Force G-4s waiting for delivery to Field Marshal Hermann Göring in 1939 at the Daimler-Benz plant at Sindelfingen, Germany. Note the small *Luftwaffe* flying eagle on the rear doors. (MB Albums, LC, Wash., DC.)

G-4 WH-32288 as it was in the former Imperial Palace Collection at Las Vegas, now dispersed worldwide, according to its former administrator, Richie Clyne, to the author. Used by Hitler in the Sudetenland in the 1960s, the car was viewed on the popular American television show *Hogan's Heroes* as Gen. Burkhalter's staff car. (Photo from the Imperial Palace Collection, Las Vegas, NV/USA.)

A good left-side view of a Sindelfingen G-4 showing the luggage storage trunk at the rear. This is *not* a *Luftwaffe* vehicle, since the door-mounted eagle is missing from the rear portal. (MB Albums, LC, Wash. DC.)

This is also *not* the same car as in the previous photo, although—at first glance—it might appear to be so! The car type and location are the same, but note the missing chrome fixture on the right front side of the luggage storage trunk at rear, and the small Air Force Nazi eagle on the right rear door near the handle, indicating that this vehicle is Reich Aviation Minister Göring's, not that of Hitler. (MB Albums, LC, Wash., DC.)

A quartet of left-side views of Hitler G-4s in front of the Sindelfingen Mercedes-Benz plant in the Third Reich. (MB Albums, LC, Wash., DC.)

Left-side views of the G-4 in "Gray Column" paint and minus the rear mudguard step. (MB Albums, LC, Wash., DC.)

Another G-4, but this one in 1938 *having* the rear mudguard step in order to facilitate getting into and out of the rear seating compartment area. (MB Albums, LC, Wash., DC.)

An excellent left-side view of a pristine G-4 ready for delivery at the Sindelfingen plant. (MB Albums, LC, Wash., DC.)

A pair of views of the same vehicle. Stated Melin, "Daimler-Benz tested the first cross-country G-4 in 1934. The design was based on the experiences that the company had had with its previous cross-country vehicle, the G-3a, but the G-4 was far too heavy and—because of this—was never really a usable, cross-country vehicle, even if it was better than, for instance, the *Grosser/Grand* Mercedes. It was, however, constantly used in parades and as a staff car." (MB Albums, LC. Wash., DC.)

This page and following: A quartet of photos showing G-4 handrails used by the *Führer* to board his vehicle by grabbing it, stepping onto the car's running board, and then hauling himself up and into it. The first shot was taken in Poland in September 1939, the rest on the Western Front in the spring of 1940. In the second view, Hitler's *SS* valet Heinz Linge is seen at the far left, while in the final scene, Hitler turns back to listen to his naval adjutant, Frigate Capt. Karl-Jesko von Puttkamer. Between them is Linge. (Photos from the Heinrich Hoffmann Albums, U.S. National Archives, College Park, MD.)

Two views of Hitler's G-4 in Berlin, in *Wehrmacht* gray war paint, with all bullet-proof windows rolled up. The wartime headlamp covers are in place as well, and the *Führerstandarte* (*Leader Flag*) is affixed. (HHA, USNA, College Park, MD/USA.)

A quartet of close-up views of Hitler's personal (and self-designed) *Führerstandarte* on the right front fenders of various G-4s, its placement when he was the ranking person present in them. When foreigners were aboard as guests, their pennants flew in the spot of honor on the right instead, a tradition from knightly, medieval times, and thus his own was as a result affixed to the left front fender. Oddly, the license plates were covered in wartime in order to conceal the identity of the famous occupant of the vehicle, but never the *Führerstandarte*! It was habitually displayed in the same fashion: inside a double-sided, weatherproof case, according to pennant expert Brian Davis. Note, too, the wartime regulation blackout lamp covers on the headlights. (HHA, USNA, College Park, MD/USA.)

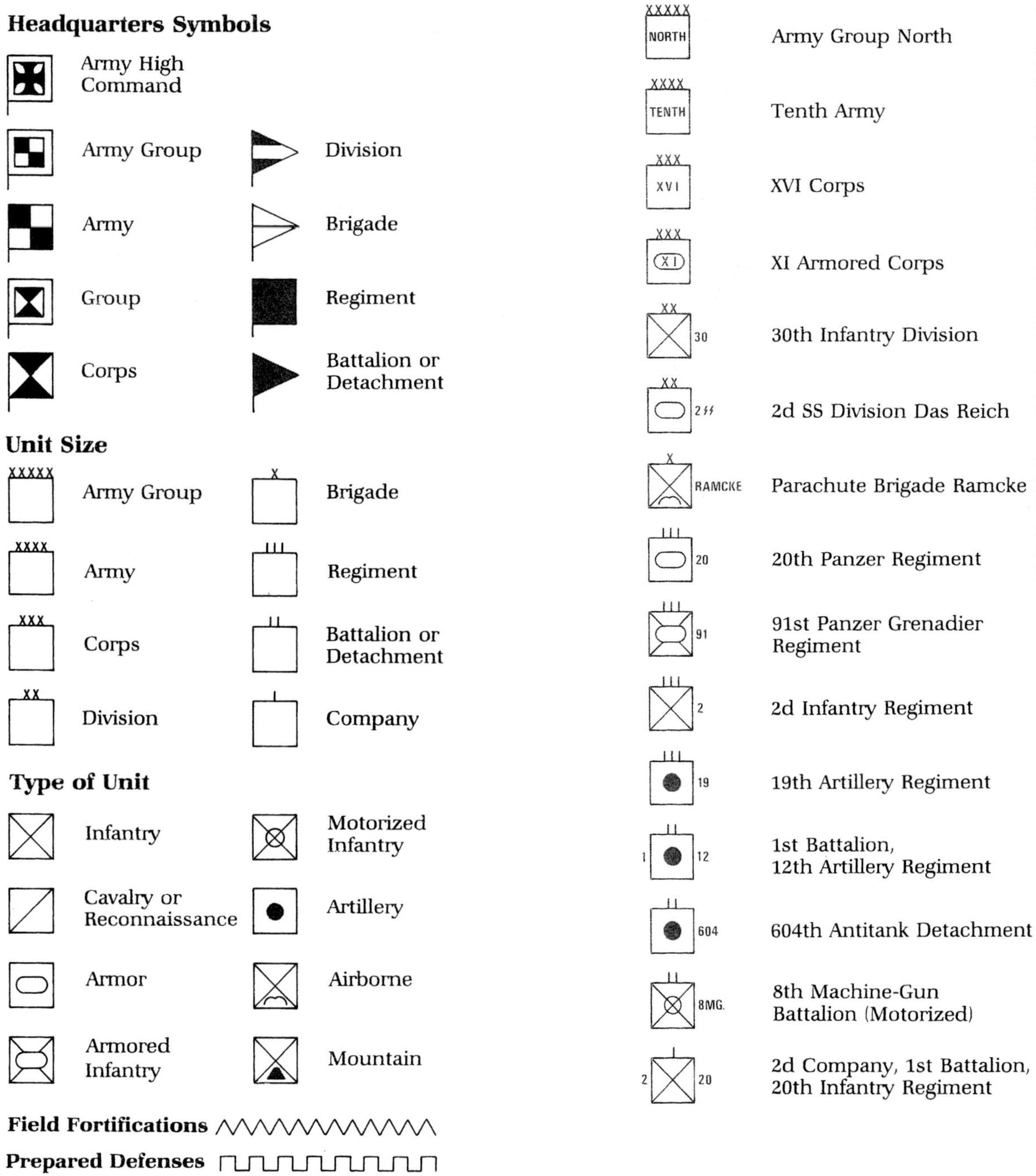

German Armed Forces map symbols used as car standards. (Courtesy Time-Life Books)

An interior view of Hitler's G-4 revealing the lush leather employed in these truly exquisite cars! Note the single-unit front and rear seating benches, and the middle seats as well—chairs, really!—complete with cushioned, upholstered armrests. The vehicle sat seven passengers comfortably. There was also an attached inset pistol holster on the right rear door. (MB Albums, LC, Wash., DC.)

The rear-mounted luggage storage trunk of the very same G-4, complete with custom-made suitcases that fit precisely in the storage area. Note, also, the blank license plate with light above, the rear and back-up lights, and the petrol cap. (MBA, LC, Wash., DC.)

The same vehicle's ornate dashboard, with handbrake at the middle on the floor. Note also the dash-mounted reading lamp at left of the open maw of the empty glove box, which—surprisingly!—has no locked cover! (MBA, LC, Wash. DC.)

The predecessor in appearance of the later G-4 was the earlier G-1, developed during 1926-28, and seen here during a road test with its two powered rear axles in use on rugged ground. Only three of these G-1 prototypes were built, one each for 1926, '27, and '28, all with six cylinder, in-line engines instead of the later eight cylinders of the G-4s. The maximum speed was 60 kph. (MBA, LC, Wash., DC.)

When standing upright in the G-4 to render his famous Nazi salutes, the *Führer* did *not* perch precariously on its front seat! Rather, the seat was folded both backwards and upwards, as displayed here, allowing Hitler to stand easily on the car's floorboard rubber mat. Note also the searchlight at upper right. (MBA, LC, Wash., DC.)

A trio of prewar road-testing shots of Göring's G-4 license plate IIA-19316 in pre-delivery views revealing its versatility. (MBA, LC, Wash., DC.)

Hermann Göring's G-4 license plate 11A-19316 of Münich registry wearing its original factory coat of dark blue paint upon delivery to its new owner, 1934. Stated author Griffith Borgeson in *Automotive Quarterly*, "But while the German generals favored the G-4 as a ceremonial car, the big six-wheeler never proved itself as a useful military vehicle. Only 70 (sic) were built." DaimlerChrysler states that but 57 were manufactured in all. (MBA, LC, Wash., DC.)

Preceded by the G-3a, the first Mercedes G-4 cross-country open tourer was road tested as early as 1934, although these amazing vehicles did not reach the public eye until the spring of 1938, with Hitler's entry into neighboring Austria during the *Anschluss* (*Union*) with the Third Reich. According to author Griffith Borgeson in *Automotive Quarterly*, "It (the G-4) was an exotic vehicle whose exceptional qualities appealed to Hitler. If his was not the first G-4 built, it was one of the first two or three. He was so satisfied with it that his next new vehicle was another G-4. It was the 1937 model, still very stylish, and now fitted with pushrod eight taken out to 5252 cc." (MBA, LC, Wash., DC.)

Occasionally, even G-4s got stuck! In length, the car was from 5500-5220mm, and its overall dimensions were 5358mm/1870mm/1900mm. The track was f/b: 1620mm/150mm. The car's tires were 7.5 x 17 low-pressure, cross-country types. (MBA, LC, Wash., DC.)

A quintet of views of the G-4 *Funkwagen* (*Radio Car*) license plate RP-700203. There was also a single *Gepackwagen* (*luggage car*) built that traveled with the *Führer* Column on several trips. (MBA, LC, Wash., DC.)

A G-4 *Luftwaffe* chassis radio car camouflaged for wartime usage. (Captured Enemy Records, USNA, College Park, MD/USA.)

The *Führer's* Reich Security Service (RSD) detail was led by Johann Rattenhuber, also known as Hans Rattenhuber in some accounts (center), seen here riding in the back seat of a Gray Column G-4 in Poland in September 1939. With Rattenhuber are some of his men, while Hitler's *SA Stormtroop* liaison officer, Gen. Wilhelm Brückner, is at far right. (HHA, USNA, College Park, MD/USA.)

A previously-unpublished, damaged print of some members of Hitler's RSD Escort with a G-4 on the Western Front in 1940. In light of the Nov. 9, 1939, Burgerbraukellar Beer Hall bomb blast, security was tightened up on the luggage carried in the cars of the Gray Column, especially in the *Führer's* own vehicle. A special directive was issued on December 14, 1939, in preparation for the coming West Front campaign to prevent the inclusion of "wrong or possibly dangerous" items in the luggage of either Hitler or his entourage—such as the "champagne bomb" planted aboard the *Führer's* plane in Russia in 1943 that failed to explode. Now all luggage was picked up by a trio of *Führer-Begleit-Battalion* (*Leader Security Battalion/FBK*) where the entourage was staying: two to get it, and one to guard the car in which it was transported. It was kept under constant guard, and never given to anyone other than an *SS-Begleit-Kommando* guard. They were the only ones designated to transport luggage to the airport—and other items brought by anyone else would not be accepted for travel. Added the directive, "Luggage that did not have to be on-hand at all times was to be stowed away in the car most distant from that in which the *Führer* traveled." (HHA, USNA, College Park. MD/USA.)

A G-4 open tourer that helped protect the *Führerkolonne* during its first invasion of a foreign country in wartime: Poland in September 1939. This is a factory shot of one of the column's security bodyguard vehicles being fitted out with protective 7.62mm MG 42 machine guns both fore and aft. Similar to the MG 34, state authors Liliane and Fred Funken in *Arms and Uniforms: The Second World War, Part 2*, "Its stronger and shorter barrel enabled it to fire more powerful ammunition." In this case, the angles of fire of the guns are being tested. (MBA, LC, Wash., DC.)

A G-4 car on escort duty for Hitler in Poland, September 1939. Noted author Peter Hoffmann in his landmark 1979 study, *Hitler's Personal Security*, the RSD men in the detail included those who'd been with him as guards for many years, and he hated to part with any of them. (MBA, LC, Wash., DC.)

An RSD G-4 security car of the *Führer* Column in Poland, September 1939, painted in wartime *Wehrmacht* gray. (HHA, USNA, College Park, MD/USA.)

A pair of similar views of the G-4 cross-country open tourers that aided in the security of the Leader Column during its invasion with Hitler of Poland in September 1939, with excellent views of the 7.62mm MG 42 machine guns at front and rear. (MBA, LC, Wash., DC.)

On June 1, 1940, Hitler's Gray Column entered the surrendered Belgian capital of Brussels from the east. According to author Jean-Paul Pallud, "From the war diary of the FHQu Commandant, we know the composition of the *FBK* convoy which toured (the city)...The first echelon comprised five motor cars, including one for Hitler, another for Keitel, one containing the ADCs, and two with security guards. The second echelon formed the motorcycle platoon under 1st Lt. Bock, the Flak platoon under 1st Lt. Rossmann, with one vehicle in reserve. Following in the third echelon under 1st Lt. Neumann were the communications team, an armored car for reconnaissance, the field kitchen, and a vehicle carrying supplies and luggage..." Here, "Having driven along Rue de la Loi and past the Palace of Justice, the convoy turned into Regency Street towards the Royal Plaza. This picture was taken just as the car was about to reach Place du Petit. The Synagogue stands on the left, the tower-like building with the Palace of Justice in the background. These vehicles are part of the first echelon, and it appears that the photographer was riding with the security guards, as an MG 34 can be seen at the ready." (HHA, USNA, College Park, MD/USA.)

Members of Hitler's well-armed RSD detail in a G-4 in Warsaw, October 5, 1939, as Hitler entered the conquered Polish capital. Sitting in the front passenger seat is *Führer* adjutant *SS* Gen. Julius Schaub, part of his so-called *chauffereska*—the inner circle of drivers, secretaries, aides, adjutants, guards, cooks, etc. that formed the team that helped Hitler function as an effective Nazi chief executive officer. Note also the headlamp cover with nighttime vertical driving slit to emit a small shaft of light. (HHA, USNA, College Park, MD/USA.)

An unusual grouping of seven of Hitler's G-4 escort cars clustered around the refueling vehicle at far right, Prague, March 15, 1939, the fabled Ides of March. (HHA, USNA, College Park, MD.)

Vehicles of the Gray Column at the *Führer's* visit to Bastogne, Belgium, to visit German Army Group A commanding officer Col. Gen. Gerd von Rundstedt, May 17, 1940. The Belgian town would become the later focal point of the Battle of the Bulge during December 1944-January 1945. (HHA, USNA, College Park, MD/USA.)

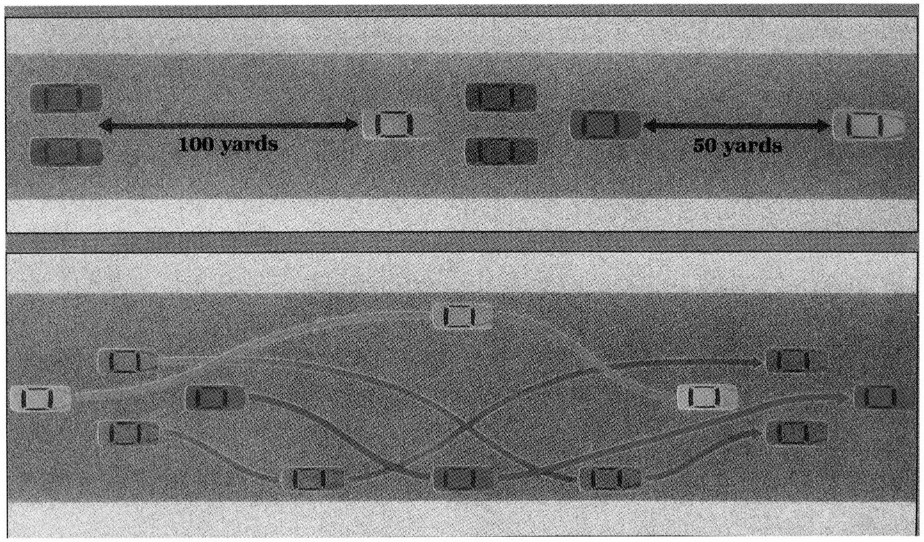

According to Time-Life Books, "The sketches…illustrate the security methods used to safeguard Hitler when he traveled by motorcade. When underway (top diagram), the *Führer's* limousine (red) was led by a pilot car (tan), 50 yards in front, and followed closely by two vehicles (green) loaded with *SS Begleit-Kommandos*, or escort guards. They, in turn, preceded an auto (orange) bearing SS officers. Any cars (blue) carrying additional VIPs followed 100 yards or more behind the convoy. Procedures for arriving, stopping, and departing are shown in the bottom diagram." (Time-Life Books.)

Two views of Hitler (right) with his final chauffeur—of three main ones—during the war at *FHQ Wolfsschanze* (*Wolf's Lair, or Ft. Wolf*), *SS* Lt. Col. Erich Kempka (1910-75), left, seen here as a major. It was he who on April 30, 1945, brought the gasoline from the *Reich Chancellery* garages in which the *Führer's* body was doused and then burned. (HHA, USNA, College Park, MD/USA.)

Hitler chauffeur *SS* Maj. Erich Kempka at the wheel of the *Führer's* G-4 in Austria, March 1938. Hitler sits in the passenger seat in the front, where he always rode unless a foreign dignitary was present; then he rode in the back with his guest. At rear can be seen a smirking German Army *OKW* (*High Command*) chief Gen. Wilhelm Keitel (left) and aide. (HHA, USNA, College Park, MD/USA.)

Hitler chauffeur *SS* Maj. Erich Kempka at the wheel of Hitler's G-4 in Ukraine during the latter's August 1941 tour in company with Italian Fascist *Duce* (*Leader*) Benito Mussolini. The *Duce*—wearing sunglasses and the uniform cap and overcoat of a Marshal of the Italian Empire—sits behind Kempka and to the left, with Hitler at right. Behind Hitler can be seen German Army Field Marshal Gerd von Rundstedt. (HHA, USNA. College Park, MD.)

Hitler's chauffeur—wearing the collar tabs of a 1st lieutenant—plays with a pet bear cub at *FHQ Wolf's Lair*, 1941. (HHA, USNA, College Park, MD/USA.)

Hitler's last of four private secretaries, Traudl Humps, married his *SS* valet, 2nd Lt. Hans Hermann Junge (center) in June 1943, accompanied by *SS* Maj. Erich Kempka (right) and Hitler's *SS* aide, 1st Lt. Otto Gunsche. (HHA, USNA, College Park, MD.)

The G-4's dashboard instruments as seen from the driver's perspective, in this case on the Weichsel River in Poland on September 22, 1939. Note, too, the thickness of the bullet-proof glass window rolled up at left. (HHA, USNA, College Park, MD/USA.)

The *Führer* disapproved of Kempka's marriage to the Hungarian-born Maja Kempka, and refused to let her live at the Berlin Chancellery. They divorced at his insistence, but lived together elsewhere. After Hitler's death and the war's end, they remarried. Here, the Kempkas (left and right), reunited postwar, are interviewed by U.S. Naval interrogator Judge Michael A. Musmanno. (Photo by Ray D'Addario, Holyoke, MA/USA.)

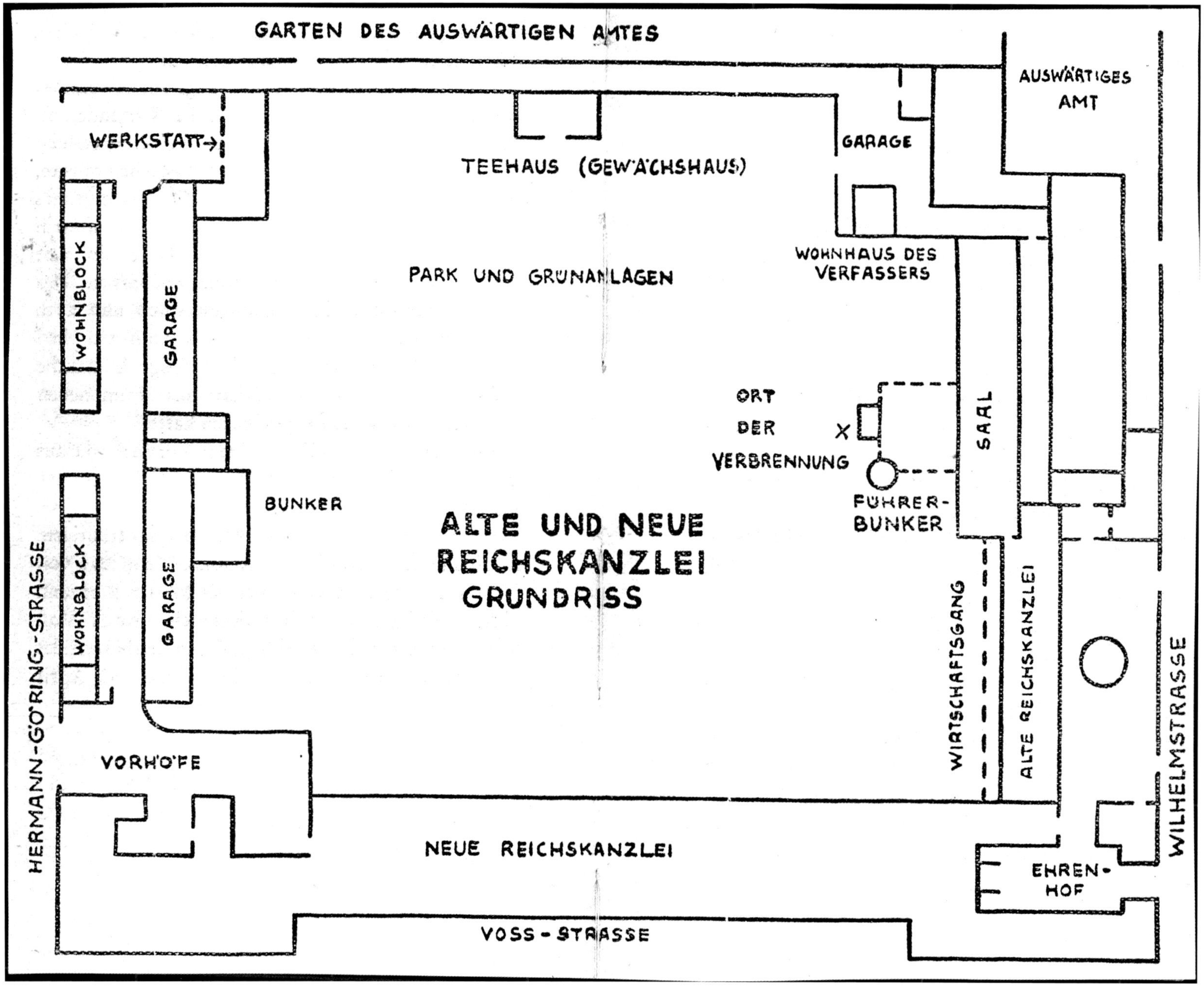

A good German map of the *New Reich Chancellery* (bottom and right) complex and the German Foreign Office (top and top right), connected by the park at center of the *Old* and *New Reich Chancelleries*, with chauffeur Kempka's garages at left, along *Hermann Göring Street*. It was in those garages that Hitler's 770K and G-4 cars were stored, as well as the gasoline that burned his body and that of his wife Eva Braun Hitler on April 30, 1945. (Author's Collection.)

Hitler wearing a rain cape and giving a casual Nazi salute—not a wave—to departing guests in a G-4 on the driveway of the *Berghof* (*Mountain Court*) during the war. (HHA, USNA, College Park, MD/USA.)

A G-4 Mercedes open tourer (right) on the Bavarian Alpine roadway built by Dr. Fritz Todt heading toward The *Berghof* in 1935. On good roads, the vehicles could achieve speeds up to 70 kph. (HHA, USNA, College Park, MD/USA.)

"At low speed, vehicle and cows seem to get along," stated this caption from the 1943 Nazi memorial biography of the late Dr. Fritz Todt, whose G-4 car this is. (HHA, USNA, College Park, MD/USA.)

"Deep holes in the limes show the evidence of thousands of years of the work of the ice. A view of the Alpine Road from the glacier garden" stated an illustrated Nazi memorial biography of Dr. Fritz Todt in 1943, completely ignoring the G-4 at top left! (HHA, USNA, College Park, MD/USA.)

Two views of Dr. Fritz Todt's own G-4 open touring car in the Bavarian Alps before the war, on the very road—the *Alpenstrasse*—built by the German engineering genius, seen standing facing the camera's lens at the center of the group outside the parked G-4. (HHA, USNA, College Park, MD/USA.)

A brace of Hitler's own G-4s—license plates IIA-19350 and IIA-19370—parked on the *Berghof* driveway in front of the structure's two-car garage, destroyed by the German government finally in 1995! Note the snow tires and their chains in place. The leather radiator cover at left is rolled up, while that at right is fully down. (HHA, USNA, College Park, MD/USA.)

G-4 license plate IIA-19370—one of Hitler's own—a Münich-registered vehicle, tests its traction in the snow on the Obersalzberg overlooking the Bavarian village of Berchtesgaden in 1934. The leather radiator cover is in the down position to keep the engine warm. (HHA, USNA, College Park, MD/USA.)

Hitler's G-4 license plate IIA-19370 full of *SS* security men from his personal bodyguard regiment—the SSLAH. Note the snow tires and chains affixed on all wheels, and the absence of "external exhaust pipes." (HHA, USNA, College Park, MD/USA.)

2

Autobahn, Military Maneuvers, *Duce* State Visit, and Austrian *Anschluss*/Union 1936-1938

According to writer Roger Shaw in the February 1939 issue of *Current Affairs* magazine in the article *Mars Motors East/The War Threat in Southeastern Europe*:

> "Last December, a 'comradely evening' was held in the vast People's Theater at Berlin. Present were 3,000 massed road laborers, full of the Yuletide—if not the Christmas—spirit. The *Führer* attended, as did the blaring brass band of his personal (SS) bodyguard, on this day of epic festivities.
>
> "These German laborers represented a State organization which has reached unprecedented importance, called the *Autobahn/Highway*. Its strategic function is to build what in America are known as motor parkways. Its Yule celebration marked completion and opening of the 3,000th kilometer of the superhighway system of the Third Reich. One purpose of this elaborate, high-speed, concrete road project is to furnish employment to the German proletariat, but the principal objective is purely military. Like the ancient roads which linked the Roman Empire, the *Autobahn* is meant to shuttle troops here and there, in a dizzy minimum of time."

Actually, during the war years of 1939-45, the German *Reichsbahn* (*Railway*) mainly fulfilled that function, but no matter:

> "The genius of the Autobahn is an unassuming German engineer named (Dr.) Fritz Todt. He was present at the Yule gathering in the People's Theater as the guest of honor. Todt it was who hastened the new German Rhineland fortifications (the *West Wall*) which face the French *Maginot Line*—those pillboxes and machine gun emplacements called by Hitler the *Limes Germanicus*.
>
> "Todt's *Autobahn* system enables the German motorist to travel from the North Sea flats to the Alpine ranges, from the industrial West to the barren 'Slavic' East, without let or hindrance. One can cover these sweeping distances without ever leaving the system, without passing through a single village or meeting a crossroad, and without any speed limit whatsoever. The *Autobahn* system consists of four lanes—two each way—and wide lanes at that. It is a veritable *Valhalla* for the Barney Oldfields of this world."

Mr. Oldfields was a famous American racing car driver of the pre-First World War era, and also during the war:

> "Todt plans to go on opening additional stretches at the rate of 1,000 kilometers, or 625 miles, per year. Hand in glove with Todt and his *Autobahn* operates the politically powerful National Socialist (Nazi) Motor Corps (*NSKK*), which—after the brown shirt Storm Troopers and the black shirt Elite (*SS*) Guards—constitutes the third branch of the Nazi Party's private army.
>
> "But German road building enterprise does not stop within the borders of the Third Reich. It extends into Germany's new dummy state of Czechoslovakia, and into that state's three autonomous, component parts: Czechy, Slovakia, and Carpatho-Ukraine. Here, too, Fritz Todt, the *Autobahn,* and the financial resources—such as they are—of the Berlin *Reichsbank/National Bank* make themselves felt. Back of this civilian energy stands the ominous figure of the old Prussian (German) General Staff.
>
> "A *German* superhighway—according to the new plans—is to cut straight through little Czechy, north to south. It will start at Breslau in German Silesia and drive straight down the map to German Vienna, thus bridging Germany's great eastern gap. This road will skirt, en route, the Czech city of Brunn. It will mean that Silesian and Austrian garrisons can be quickly motorized up and down the Eastern Front, or pushed into the long runway of Czechoslovakia for a drive toward the Orient, or the Polish and Soviet Ukrainian regions Also, of course—from a commercial point of view—the Breslau-Vienna parkway will prove itself a godsend.
>
> "Germany will pay for this highway, and will have complete judicial sovereignty over it, enjoying full extra-territorial rights. It will be a German corridor through the Czechs, similar to Uncle Sam's Canal Zone, which cuts arbitrarily through the so-called Republic of Panama. And just as Panama's Presidential cabinets had better be pro-American, so, too, the present Czechoslovak cabinet is markedly pro-German. German citizens will need no passports in the projected Czech corridor, nor will there be any customs inspection for loaded trucks and lorries.
>
> "But this is only the beginning of Todt and the *Autobahn* among the Czechs, Slovaks, and Carpatho-Ukrainians. Down the whole length of Czechoslovakia, the Prague government plans to run another superhighway, from west to far east. It will give jobs to an estimated 50,000-100,000 workmen, and—except for iron ore—all the necessary materials are at hand. Completion may take five or six years, but if Todt takes an active part in the job, it will go through considerably faster.

"Says the *Prager Presse* [*Prague Press*] enthusiastically, 'The first steps to execution of the project—which are being taken immediately—show the path which the Second Republic of Czechoslovakia wishes to tread. For the new highway from west to east will be the first big modern motor road in Central Europe, and will thus link up the Republic with the great traffic network which surrounds it.'

"To put things as simply as possible, German troops can motor into Czechoslovakia by the Breslau-Vienna corridor project, and then can chug along east on the full-length Czechoslovak high-speed route. (Which, in fact, they did on March 15, 1939, the month after this article was first published, when Hitler occupied the entire country.)

"This leads straight to the Rumanian frontier. Rumania is the goal, due to her rich oil wells and poor geography. For southeast through Rumania lies the way to the Black Sea and the important coastal city of Odessa in the Soviet Union: a primary Nazi objective. In short, all roads lead to the Ukraine—with its wheat, its minerals, and its seething, under-surface discontent." (As, indeed, the invading German armies discovered on June 22, 1941, when Hitler invaded the USSR as well.)

"Motor-minded and military minded, Adolf Hitler plans an army on wheels. If a Russo-German war comes, automobiles will play an important part: tanks, armored cars, trucks, staff carriers, gun tractors, and the like. Both the Red and German armies know this, and are preparing for it. Infantry will be motorized for speedy transport, and supported by light whippets and steel-plate juggernauts. Artillery will be hauled by machines, or loaded on them. Field kitchens will be motor-drawn.

"The Nazis fully understand that Mars (the God of War) is now in the motor age. The entire German automobile industry has been totalized for military needs, with an accompanying standardization of trucks and passenger cars.

"All German truck manufacturers now will produce three uniform standard models: 1 1/2–ton, 3-ton, and 5-ton machines. 'In each category, Col. (Adolf) von Schell will select the model best suited for its dual military and civil functions,' trumpets Berlin.

"This process would seem to eliminate capitalist competition, and Germany still claims to be capitalistic, but the government has an answer to that. The various concerns will present competitive plans for each standard model, and the winner will be allowed to charge the other companies production royalties. This means a clean up for the initiator of each standard truck type. No fancy gadgets or swanky bourgeois (middle class) refinements will be tolerated in the passenger cars. Instead of 135 different automobile models—as at present—there will be 15 types only, all designed for military as well as private use. The manufacturers will be forced to maintain each model for several years, and to combine speed, simplicity, and ruggedness. The big Mercedes six-wheeler the (G-4)—Hitler entered Vienna in one of these cross-country sports cars—is a favored 'Schell' type. Motorcycles are also a popular German weapon, and there is so large a stock of them that the entire army could be moved on two wheels if it were desired. Germany has three armored, mechanized army divisions totaling perhaps 30,000 men, and is believed to be forming one more. Up to this year, she had had only a single brigade of horse cavalry. This, primarily, was to keep the rough-riding younger sons of the East Prussian Junkers happy. However, additional horse cavalry is now being created for use on the flat steppes of the east."

In the actual event of war, however, as of Sept. 1, 1939, Hitler's invasion of Poland also meant the abrupt end of all private passenger car production in the Third Reich for the rest of its life, until May 8, 1945. The article was dead wrong on the cavalry issue, though, as the non-equestrian *Führer* was then busily eliminating the famed cavalry arm of the German Army, only to reform it by necessity *after* his disastrous invasion of the Soviet Union:

"The German Army consists of 42 fairly good, first-line divisions, very short on artillery; six poor divisions from the former Austrian Army; two good reserve divisions in East Prussia; and 38 reserve divisions lacking artillery, motor transport, and suitable staff officers. This reaches a total of perhaps a million men—'too many Viennese chocolate soldiers, not enough Mecklenburg giants'—as a home critic put it. The essential weakness in reserves is accounted for by the fact that the Reich was forbidden to utilize conscription between 1919-35. In the latter year, it was readopted for a two-year period, plus a preparatory six-months Labor Service on public works like the *Autobahn*.

"But if Germany heads toward the Soviet Ukraine and the Ukrainian minority of Poland in a prospective automobile war, what of the motorization in the Russian Red Army—'the bear that walks like a man, with its head shot off'—according to one wit? Certainly the brains of the Red Army—due to Stalin's purgings—are in the grave.

"Nevertheless, the industrial brains of the Soviet Union have kept buzzing along automotive lines. Here, new models in cars and trucks have been introduced to counter the threat from Todt and Schell. The Stalin plant at Moscow, for instance, is preparing for mass production of a seven-seater open car, plus a six-passenger closed job dated 1937.

"This new machine has a radio, heater, folding top, and luggage compartment, and can do 75 miles per hour." (Stalin's *own* G-4 knock-off? Maybe.)

"Russia's automobile industry dates back to 1924, when the Stalin plant turned out 10 1 ½-ton trucks, largely by hand. Today, this auto factory employs 40,000 workers, and occupies 1,000 acres of ground. It hopes to enlarge to an annual capacity of 100,000 3-ton trucks and 16,000 passenger cars. It turns out a 27-passenger streamlined bus—excellent for military purposes—with even bigger and better buses in the offing.

"The Moscow works, largest in all Russia, manufactured 130,000 machines last year, including 17,000 passenger cars. The Molotov and the Stalin combined, accounted for 200,000 machines and $70,000,000 worth of spare parts.

"Russia's Ukrainian and Manchurian fronts are 8,000 miles apart, and rail communications are defective. Hence, automobiles are prime necessities for the Red Army. The Trans-Siberian Railway has been double-tracked, it is true, and there is a new Baikul-Amur rail line in the Far East, but it is on the strategic auto routes that the Red Army primarily depends for defense against Hitler. It could hardly take the offensive in its present state, according to competent military critics. It creaks when it laboriously moves, hence the speedup in automobile production.

"Not all automobile races are held on the Indianapolis motor speedway. There the Fiats, Peugeots, Sunbeams, and Stutzes used to race one another before perhaps 100,000 people The *new* automobile contest may be a road race of Mercedes against Molotov, with a higher death rate than the Indianapolis '500 mile' ever saw. As its audience—cheering or booing loudly—may sit the 2 billion inhabitants of the globe."

In its May 1937 issue, *Current History* had run an article by Frank C. Hanighen entitled *Germany's New Roads: Are these Nazi highways designed for the traffic of tourists or war tanks?* The answer to the latter part of the question was an emphatic "No!" at least not as concerned their heavy steel treads meeting concrete. Some excerpts follow:

"It should be mentioned that the German staff has recently felt some doubt about the value of the present highway planning in view of the experience in the Spanish war (of 1936-39). In Spain, the magnificent highways constructed by (Gen.) Primo de Rivera have been so conspicuous that they have been easy marks for attacks by both rebel and Loyalist planes, and as a result much traffic has sought the comparative safety of the smaller side roads. The Germans, therefore, have been reconsidering the nature of the whole *Autobahn* program, and it is likely that the smaller, side roads in Germany will receive more attention…

"The most remarkable fact about Germany's motorization program, however, is not the extensive building of roads, but the amazing increase in the production of motor vehicles. Germany has jumped from fifth position among the world's auto producers in 1932 (U.S. first, Britain second, France third, Canada fourth) to third place in 1935, with only the U.S. and Britain leading her. In 1932, Germany had but one motor vehicle to 100 inhabitants. In 1935, it had one to 59. Still a long way from the US with one to five, it is nevertheless rapidly advancing toward France's figure, which has hovered around 22 for several years.

"This extraordinary increase did not arise from the laws of demand and supply, but from a systematic program of subsidy and assistance to the motor industry. The Nazi government immediately on entering office pushed a program of 'more motorcars.' All public officials were subjected to constant propaganda and pressure to buy cars—or, if they possessed old cars, to replace them with new. Traffic policemen had orders to stop drivers of old cars and to urge them as a patriotic duty to buy new ones. So much for the work of the propaganda leader Göbbels! …Germany's new motor roads are viewed with suspicion; however, it has even been suggested that the Germans built them for pleasure and convenience…."

Duce

On Heroes' Memorial Day in Berlin on March 15, 1935, Chancellor Hitler unilaterally abrogated the 1919 Versailles Treaty that limited Germany's national army to but 100,000 men, and at the same time announced that he was re-instituting a universal draft for all German males of military age, effective immediately. This new army of conscripts brought in its train annual military maneuvers each September during 1935-38 of the Army and Air Force. During Italian Fascist Party *Duce* Benito Mussolini's State Visit to Nazi Germany in 1937, he was Hitler's guest of honor at that year's events.

It was at these Mecklenburg maneuvers in September 1937 that the new Axis team of *Führer* and *Duce* arrived in one of Hitler's spanking new G-4s, their first public appearance.

Anschluss

Then came the Nazi "union" with Austria in March-April 1938, as detailed in English author Gordon Brook-Shepherd's 1963 work *The Anschluss*, in which Hitler re-entered his native land in a massive G-4, thus introducing this splendid vehicle to the world at large via newsreels that are still shown in documentaries today:

"It was not until 10 minutes to four in the afternoon (of March 12, 1938) that the *Führer* finally crossed the border at his birthplace, Braunau-am-Inn (River.) If the delay had been caused to any extent by lingering doubts about the reception awaiting him, these were swept away the moment his open Mercedes-Benz car reached the frontier bridge, which—until that morning—had linked two independent countries. The troop columns that had entered before him had marched—brass bands out at the front and ammunition trains left far behind in Germany—along roads lined with cheering crowds. The arrival of Hitler himself turned this enthusiasm into frenzy, and the frenzy mounted to a fateful climax as the procession of cars made its way from Braunau across the rolling countryside of Upper Austria, through Ried and Wels, and so into the streets of the provincial capital.

"At Linz—as everywhere along the route—there were also some who stayed, silent and bitter, in their homes. As everywhere, not every uplifted arm meant an uplifted heart, but of the 120,000 people that the city numbered at the time, 100,000 must've been out to watch the *Führer* arrive at 8 o'clock in the evening, and neither Hitler nor the photographers needed to look beyond the outstretched arms. Driven partly by genuine Nazi and pan-German fanaticism and partly by the mass hysteria of this dramatic moment, the town went wild and produced a welcome that was more Oriental than European in flavor. On this part of the story, the descriptions circulated by Göbbels' team of propaganda writers tallied with the accounts of all foreign observers present."

Indeed, it was at Linz's Hotel Weinzinger that Hitler decided that night to annex Austria outright to the Third Reich, without having first entered the former Habsburg capital of Vienna. Rejoins Brook-Shepherd:

"It was soon after 5 o'clock in the afternoon of Monday, March 14th that the *Führer* entered Vienna—a tense, unsmiling figure…standing bolt upright in his open car—the right hand outstretched in salute, the left gripping the top of the windscreen. The 120-mile journey from Linz had taken over six hours, a snail's procession caused partly by the loyal addresses and the cascades of flowers en route, but partly by the traffic chaos on the road as SS vehicles tried to leap-frog the broken down lorries of Gen. Fedor von Bock's mechanized regiments. The first dress rehearsal of the new *Wehrmacht/Armed Forces* had not, in fact, gone at all smoothly, and this accounted for the mixed temper in which the *Führer* arrived.

"Vienna's welcome was perhaps less concentrated that that of Linz…yet the sheer numbers involved made the setting even more spectacular…"

Following is author Evan Burr Bukev's account of those same Nazi motorcades from his 2000 work *Hitler's Austria: Popular Sentiment in the Nazi Era 1938-45:*

"The *Führer* crossed the Inn River at Braunau. The streets were so choked by cheering crowds that Hitler's chauffeur (Kempka) had to downshift his three-axle, cross-country (G-4) open Mercedes to avoid injuring the well-wishers. To the tune of peeling bells and thunderous applause, the motorcade proceeded to Linz, arriving at 7:30 PM. When Hitler stepped onto the Rathaus balcony to address the throng, between 60-80,000 Austrians roared their approval….

"The vast crowds welcoming the invading *Wehrmacht* were not without influence. Hitler had originally envisioned a 'personal union' of Germany and Austria, but he was so moved by his hometown reception that the following afternoon—Sunday, March 13, 1938—he signed a law incorporating his native land into the German Reich….

"On Monday, March 14, 1938, Hitler left Linz. His motorcade proceeded along the fabled *Nibelungenstrasse/Nibelung Street,* driving through crowds chanting Nazi slogans and shouting '*Sieg Heil!'/Hail Victory!* Two and a half hours later, the dictator paused at Melk to take the salute of the local Austrian garrison. After another stop at St. Polten, his procession slowed to 20 kilometers an hour to please the howling masses.

"At 5:40 PM, the *Führer's* Mercedes swung onto Vienna's *Ringstrasse* to the sound of cheers and peeling bells. The correspondent of the *Manchester Guardian* reported that the Imperial boulevard was so densely lined with spectators that 'The German police and SA—who had kept order along the route—had to make repeated efforts to keep back the crowd, which often broke through at different places.'

"Accompanied by two dozen police cars, Hitler's motorcade swept past the Gothic Rathaus, the classical Greek Parliament, the Museums of Art and Natural History, the Hofburg, and the State Opera. At the Hotel Imperial—once home to (composer) Richard Wagner (Hitler's hero), it came to a halt. Here the conqueror of Vienna stepped from the running board to receive Dr. Artur Seyss-Inquart's cabinet.

"G.E.R. Gedye described the 'roaring crowds' as 'the greatest I have ever seen in Vienna.'"

Here is another account from the *Führer's* longtime photographer, Reich Photo Reporter Prof. Heinrich Hoffmann, in his 1955 memoir, *Hitler was my Friend*:

"At the beginning of March 1938…he suddenly turned to me and said, 'Hoffmann, I've got a small conference in Muhldorf. Would you like to come with me? …Above all, don't forget to bring your Leica!' (camera.) In Muhldorf—not far from the Austrian frontier—Hitler went straight to the village school, where he was received by a number of general officers.

"On the tables, I noticed that large scale General Staff maps had been spread out. Now what—maneuvers—and at this time of year? I had heard, of course, that troops had been concentrated on the frontier, in order to impress the gravity of the situation on the Austrian government; but at the same time, I had also heard that the whole thing was a bluff.

"When Hitler left the school, he was in high spirits. 'Gentlemen,' he said, 'how would you like to accompany me to Simbach? It's only a few miles away, and I would dearly like to have a look at my birthplace, Braunau, which is on the opposite bank of the Inn.'

"As we drove into Simbach, it was obvious that Hitler was expected. Flags and banners with slogans flew everywhere, and workmen were working furiously to complete the decorations of some of the streets and houses. A roar of cheering greeted our arrival. Suddenly, Hitler stood up in the car. He drew himself stiffly to attention. 'Now—over the bridge and into Braunau!' he ordered.

"In the middle of the bridge—the Austro-German frontier—a German officer stood waiting. Little children in festive garb surrounded the car, offering their bouquet of flowers to the *Führer.* It was only then that we realized what the people of Simbach already knew—we were off to Austria!

"Hitler turned round and laughed joyously at our surprised faces. Another surprise packet had come off! Braunau was in a turmoil of excitement, and it was now for the first time that we heard that, hours before, German troops had crossed the frontier, and had everywhere been greeted with tremendous enthusiasm.

"We wondered where on earth the population had got hold of those masses of swastika flags, photos of Hitler, and slogan-bearing banners, all of which were forbidden in Austria, under pain of heavy penalty

"Standing on the running board of the *Führer's* car, I started to record the enthusiasm of the crowd with my Leica. The camera does not lie, and the films prove conclusively that, in 1938, the overwhelming majority of the Austrian population was in favor of Adolf Hitler and the *Anschluss/Union* with Germany.

"Hour after hour the cries of '*Heil/Hail!'* rang in our ears, and wherever the *Führer's* car stopped for an instant, enthusiasm rose to a tornado of cheers."

Added August Kubizek in his book, *The Young Hitler I Knew,* the *Führer* returned to his homeland at exactly the spot where his late father had once worked as an Imperial Austrian Customs official.

Finally, there are these observations of Dr. Peter Hoffmann in his 1979 work *Hitler's Personal Security*:

"Hitler's trip to Austria in March 1938 can hardly count as one to a foreign country: it was his homeland, and in the process of being occupied by the *Wehrmacht*. But although there was no active Austrian military resistance, Hitler's trip to Linz and Vienna was—from a security point of view—much like one to a foreign country."

The overall *SS/RSD/FBK* security detail numbered 31:

"Ten of them were drivers, including their leader, Kempka. Two, including Hitler's later SS adjutant, Otto Gunsche, were responsible for the luggage…At least five cars were necessary to carry the entire crew of bodyguards and their weapons and luggage, and additional cars carried Hitler and (his) constant companions…making up a convoy of more than 12 cars, all of them Mercedes-Benz.

"Hitler used a G-4 three-axle, cross-country Mercedes bearing the Army license plate WH-32290." After his arrival at Braunau on March 12th, the *Führer* "Went on to Lambach, Wels, and Linz. The masses cheered endlessly, the delays were stupefying. The night was spent in Linz, and on March 13th the journey continued on to Vienna. Up to St. Polten, the average speed of the convoy was 40 kilometers per hour.

"Hitler's progress through Austria was nothing short of triumphal, and much of the enthusiasm encountered was undoubtedly genuine…although it was considerably less universal in industrial centers than elsewhere [reflecting his rural appeal].

"At a crossroads between Linz and Melk—where the road turns off toward Vienna—Mason-MacFarlane stopped for petrol at a garage and learned, on March 13th, that Hitler was about to pass by, and he decided to wait for the spectacle. Presently, two Mercedes cars 'filled with SS bristling with tommy-guns and other lethal weapons, came by; they were closely followed by half a dozen super cars containing Hitler and his immediate entourage and bodyguard.'

"The trip was completed without serious incidents."

Area schoolboys hang onto the doors of a G-4 on Dr. Todt's Alpine Road before the war. (Todt archives, USNA, College Park, MD/USA.)

Note the G-4 at right in the *Führer's* motorcade during the opening of one of the German *Autobahns*. (HHA, USNA, College Park, MD/USA.)

His personal G-4 parked on the roadside, Hitler (center) chats with German Army Commander-in-Chief Gen. Werner von Fritsch in September 1935, while *SS* bodyguard Karl Wilhelm Krause (still living) is seen standing between them at rear by the car. *SS* chauffeur Erich Kempka is at the wheel. Note the SA unit at right, its pennant visible on the flagstaff just behind license plate 11A-19350. The pennant at far right denotes a detachment, while the *Führerstandarte* on the mudguard is Hitler's own. (HHA, USNA, College Park, MD.)

The *Führer's* G-4 on maneuvers in the field, with a trio of Naval officers in back. (HHA, USNA, College Park, MD/USA.)

The German Army's annual military maneuvers took place each fall. Here is G-4 license plate 11A-19350, a Münich-registered car, with Hitler sitting up front beside *SS* chauffeur Col. Julius Schreck (1898-1936). The officers behind Hitler are unknown. (HHA, USNA, College Park, MD/USA.)

A line of G-4s on military maneuvers, September 1935. License plate 11A-19350—Hitler's own—heads up the group. (HHA, USNA, College Park, MD.)

As it was so heavy, the G-4 (chassis #105184) often got stuck, as witness 11A-19350 here, in 1935, as Hitler stands by—third from left—waiting for it to be dug out of the mud by members of his escort squad. (HHA, USNA, College Park, MD/USA.)

Saluted by two Navy sailors with their rifles at port arms, Hitler leaves a local Naval headquarters, heading for his waiting G-4 at right, license plate 11A-19350. *SS* bodyguard Karl Wilhelm Krause waits at the door; maneuvers, September 1935. (Previously-unpublished photo, HHA, USNA, College Park, MD/USA.)

During the September 1935 annual fall military maneuvers, the Reich Chancellor (center) shakes hands with Ambassador to England Joachim von Ribbentrop, wearing *SS* uniform at left, next to Hitler's G-4 at right flying the *Führerstandarte* on the left fender. At rear is a car of Hitler's prewar *Sonderzug* (*Special Train*). (Joachim von Ribbentrop Albums, USNA, College Park, MD/USA.)

A rare view of Hitler's G-4—license plate I IA-19350—at left and German Army C-in-C Gen. Werner von Fritsch's G-4 at right, complete with Army High Command standard on its own left fender. In the group at rear, Hitler is at left and von Fritsch at right with the September 1935 military maneuver umpires, wearing light-colored bands around their peaked caps. (Previously-unpublished photo, HHA, USNA, College Park, MD/USA.)

On Sept. 26, 1937—sitting in the rear seats—Italian Fascist *Duce* Benito Mussolini (left) and his host, Hitler, at right arriving in the *Führer's* G-4 at Mecklenburg for the fall German military maneuvers. The *Duce's* Fascist Party *fasces* pennant is affixed on the right front mudguard. Note the dirt on the tires, making them appear as whitewalls—they are *not*! (HHA, USNA, College Park, MD/USA.)

A close-up of the G-4's passengers, from left to right: unknown German Army officer, Mussolini, Hitler, a second unidentified German Army officer giving a military salute, and SS chauffeur Erich Kempka at the wheel, Mecklenburg, Sept. 26, 1937. (HHA, USNA. College Park, MD/USA.)

Both the German and Italian delegations at the fall military maneuvers of the German Army, Mecklenburg, Sept. 26, 1937. Note the *Führer's* G-4 parked at top right of the picture, and the standards of both the *Duce* and Hitler held by the German soldiers at far left. Mussolini and the *Führer* stand at far right. (HHA, USNA, College Park, MD/USA.)

German (left) and Austrian (right) border guards tear down the boundary post between the two countries as German troops enter peacefully on March 12, 1938. As noted by Canadian author Prof. Peter Hoffmann in his superb 1979 work *Hitler's Personal Security,* "The mayor of Muhldorf…wandered around, trying to find out what was up. Finally, he saw someone taking the *Führer's* Standard off the black Mercedes and putting it on a G-4 Mercedes painted in Army drab. Someone in Hitler's suite said, 'The *Führer* is going to Braunau.'" Hitler crossed into Austria following German Army units that had preceded him that day, Saturday, March 12, 1938, in G-4 license plate WH-32290 at his birthplace, *Braunau-am-Inn* (Braunau on the River Inn). (HHA, USNA, College Park, MD/USA.)

The *Führer* (left) gives a casual, back-handed Nazi salute (and *not* a wave, as some writers assert) as he enters the Austrian village of Melk on Monday, March 14, 1938, with its famed Benedictine Abbey seen in the distance on the Danube River, "as a tourist to visit the grave of his mother," as Hermann Göring cynically told the international diplomatic corps in Berlin. Here, unable to control herself, one Austrian girl bursts into tears as his G-4 approaches her. (HHA, USNA, College Park, MD/USA.)

Hitler at Braunau on Sunday, March 13, 1938, in G-4 license plate WH-32290. The WH stood for *Wehrmacht Heer* (Armed Forces Army). In the first view, Hitler's car overtakes the lead armored car of the *LSSAH Hitler Bodyguard Regiment* in the car on wet cobblestones. In the final shot, Hitler stops briefly to accept a bouquet of flowers, a road map clutched under his left arm, with the head and peaked cap of German Army *Ritter* (*Knight*) von Schobert seen just below that., while *SS* adjutant Julius Schaub holds another floral garland in the right rear of the car. Wrote German Army Field Marshal Wilhelm Keitel in his jail cell at Nurnberg in late 1946, as he awaited hanging, "We drove through Adolf Hitler's birthplace, Braunau, acclaimed by the townsfolk with an unending roar of welcome" and were later "delayed in every town and village on the way by advancing troops and the wildly cheering crowds that packed around us…The atmosphere of the whole demonstration was electric and excited beyond belief. I had never seen anything like it before, and I was deeply impressed…A reception like this was something I had never dreamed of." The motorcade included 12 Mercedes-Benz cars in all. (HHA, USNA, College Park, MD/USA.)

Hitler's G-4 pulls up before the Hotel Weinzinger in Linz, Austria, on March 12, 1938, where he decided to annex Austria outright to Nazi Germany, based on his triumphant reception thus far that day by the populace. He returned again to the hotel on 8 April during an election campaign to convince the Austrian people to ratify his decision; they did. (HHA, USNA, College Park, MD/USA.)

The *Führer's* G-4 surrounded by mobs of adoring Austrians during his triumphant entry of Melk on Monday, March 14, 1938. (HHA, USNA, College Park, MD/USA.)

Hitler greets his boyhood history teacher at Linz, Austria, March 12, 1938. Between them can be seen *SS* bodyguard Karl Wilhelm Krause. (HHA, USNA, College Park, MD/USA.)

The *Führer's* G-4 license plate WH-32290 in front of his boyhood home where his late parents lived in Leonding, Austria, Sunday, March 13, 1938, Michaelsbergstrasse 16. (HHA, USNA, College Park, MD/USA.)

On Sunday, March 13, 1938, Hitler visited his parents' graves at Leonding after an absence of 25 years since he'd left Austria in 1913 (to move to Münich for good), and is seen here leaving the churchyard for his G-4, followed by, from left to right *SA Führer* aide Wihelm Brückner, *SS* bodyguard Karl Wilhelm Krause, press chief Dr. Otto Dietrich, Martin Bormann, *Luftwaffe* Gen. Karl Bodenschatz, and an RSD man at the car itself awaiting him. He wanted to leave Linz for Vienna right away, but accepted instead the combined advice of his *SS* security chiefs—Heinrich Himmler and Reinhard Heydrich—to delay his arrival there until Monday, 14 March, because security wasn't yet ready for him. (HHA, USNA, College Park, MD/USA.)

An ebullient *Führer* leans out of his G-4 to touch the head of a well-wisher. Note the direction turn indicator at far right, mounted on the doorframe just below the windshield. (HHA, USNA, College Park, MD/USNA.)

One car, two Chancellors: at left is that of Austria, Nazi lawyer Artur von Seyss-Inquart (1892-1946), and Hitler of Germany at right, both in G-4 license plate WH-32290, March 14, 1938. (HHA, USNA, College Park, MD/USA.)

Another view of Hitler's arrival at Linz, Austria—a city he later decided would house art museums to rival those of Paris—at 8 PM on Saturday, March 12, 1938, with Hitler up front next to *SS* chauffeur Erich Kempka at the wheel. On the jump seat behind is German Army Gen. Gerd von Rundstedt (in the seat usually held by *SS* guard Karl Wilhelm Krause), while Krause himself sits in the left rear seat of the G-4. German Army troops hold back cheering Austrians. (HHA, USNA, College Park, MD/USA.)

Hitler drives into Linz, Austria, at 8 PM on March 12, 1938, in G-4 license plate WH-32290. Note the frantic RSD men clearing a path from both left and right for the G-4, as a photographer scampers out of the path of the oncoming car! The reception that Hitler received in Linz—by 100,000 cheering Austrians—as the G-4 made its way to the Town Hall convinced Hitler then and there, he later said, to annex Austria outright to the Third Reich as soon as possible. (HHA, USNA, College Park, MD/USA.)

SS bodyguard Karl Wilhelm Krause stands behind Hitler to intercept the bouquet of flowers being handed to the *Führer* from the happy woman being restrained by the Austrian helmeted civilian at right as Hitler enters Linz on Saturday, March 12, 1938. Krause—nicknamed *Hitlers Schatten (Hitler's Shadow)*—sat in the mid-car jump seat directly behind Hitler in the G-4, and also walked immediately behind him to guard his back. (HHA, USNA, College Park, MD/USA.)

Hitler's grand entry into the former Imperial Austrian Habsburg capital city of Vienna, Monday, March 14, 1938. Kempka is at the wheel of G-4 license plate WH-32290, and Austrian Chancellor Artur von Seyss-Inquart rides in the jump seat at mid-car just behind the Nazi *Führer*. Walking at far right at the car's fender is RSD chief Johann Rattenhuber. (HHA, USNA, College Park, MD/USA.)

Another view of the same event, in my view one of the more dramatic scenes from Hitler's life ever photographed, with his massive G-4 at front and center. The statue at rear is of Austrian Archduke Karl. (HHA, USNA, College Park, MD/USA.)

RFSS Heinrich Himmler (right) is greeted as he arrives in Vienna ahead of Hitler, March 1938, to establish security. Note the G-4 behind him. (Photo from the Hugo Jager Collection, LC, Wash., DC.)

On March 28, 1938, *Luftwaffe* Field Marshal Hermann Göring raises his baton at Wiener-Neustadt airport in Austria. The G-4 is license plate 1A-103727. (Previously-unpublished photo from the Hermann Göring Albums, LC, Wash., DC.)

Riding in G-4 license plate 1A-103727—a Berlin-registered car—Göring crosses the Reich Bridge in Vienna on March 26, 1938, during the plebescite election campaign in Austria to ratify Hitler's occupation of two weeks earlier. His G-4 is followed by open tourers, among which is a Mercedes Type 320 at right, while at left are parked *Luftwaffe* staff cars and saluting German Regular Police. The banner over the bridge at rear reads, "A hail to victory of the SA for our General Göring," ignoring by mistake his rank as a Marshal! (HGA, LC, Wash., DC.)

Göring in Vienna, March 26, 1938, riding next to his *SS* chauffeur, behind whom, in the G-4's mid-car jump seat is Austrian Chancellor Artur von Seyss-Inquart (now wearing black *SS* uniform). Behind him is Gen. Karl Bodenschatz (right) and Nazi *Gauleiter* (Regional Leader) of Rhine-Pfalz (left rear) Josef Burckel, appointed by Hitler on April 23, 1938, as Reich Commissar of Austria. (HGA, LC, Wash., DC.)

On the same day—March 26, 1938—Hermann Göring rides into Wiener-Neustadt (Vienna New City) in the same G-4 (but now Göring wears an overcoat), and returns the salute of Austrian Army troops with his ornate Marshal's baton. Behind Göring on the jump seat is Air Force Gen. Hans-Jurgen Stumpf. On the mudguards are his car pennants: (left) the Marshal's flag and (right) that of the Nazi Party .The car is license plate IA-103727. (Previously-unpublished photo, HGA, LC, Wash., DC.)

Hermann Göring (left) as a politician greets a baby from his G-4 on April 1, 1938, at Mauterndorf, Austria, whose castle he would later acquire as his own. The car is license plate 1A-103727. (Previously-unpublished photo by Helmuth Kurth, HGA, LC, Wash., DC.)

Field Marshal Hermann Göring rides to the reviewing stand in just-occupied Vienna on March 15, 1938, to review the Nazi parade of the Austrian Army, riding in Mercedes-Benz G-4 license plate 1A-103727, a Berlin-registered vehicle. He salutes from the right front passenger seat with his *Luftwaffe* baton, at the side of his *SS* chauffeur, behind whom rides his aide Paul "Pilli" Körner in *SS* black on the jump seat. Behind him is Gen. Karl Bodenschatz. (Previously-unpublished photo by Helmuth Kurth, HGA, LC, Wash., DC.)

On March 30, 1938, Hermann Göring makes another election campaign trip into what the Nazis called the *Österreich* (*Eastern Province*), and is greeted upon his arrival at the village of Bleiberg by the local populace and Nazis. This time, Göring wears traditional South German dress, and his G-4 is decorated with oak leaves, the German symbol for a victorious conqueror. The car is license plate 1A-103727. (Previously-unpublished photo by Helmuth Kurth, HGA, LC, Wash., DC.)

3

Czechoslovakia and the West Wall 1938-39

As I wrote in my first book in 1993 (*Guarding the Führer: Sepp Dietrich, Johann Rattenhuber and the Protection of Adolf Hitler*):

"Back in the now expanded Third Reich, the *Führer* planned his next move, *Operation Gruhn/Green,* the proposed German invasion of Czechoslovakia, again pairing the successful team of (Heinz) Guderian- (Sepp) Dietrich.

"...War with the West looked imminent...The Münich Conference (of Sept. 30, 1938) took place instead; with war averted, Hitler had been given the German-speaking Sudetenland for free...Six months later—during a blinding snowstorm—the *Leibstandarte/Lifeguard* took part in the *Führer's* occupation of the rest of Czechoslovakia with Gen. Erwin Rommel in charge of security once the drive on Prague began."

Added British revisionist historian David Irving in his 1978 work *The War Path: Hitler's Germany 1933-39*:

"He (Hitler) left Berlin on Oct. 2, 1938 with Brauchitsch, Milch, and Todt for a flying tour of the newly regained Sudeten lands—he was being cheered by tumultuous crowds in the ancient market places of Asch and Eger, and standing amidst the lines of now-abandoned Czech fortifications: all this his propaganda machine had won for him...

"As Hitler drove on from Asch and Eger in a column of three-axled cars packed with SS, Henlein's officials and the Party...some towns looked as if a full-scale war had hit them: buildings were wrecked, telephone lines were down, there was broken glass everywhere, food queues and mobile food kitchens...Hitler's thoughts were never far from the unconquered bulk of Czechoslovakia, of which Chamberlain and Münich had, he considered, temporarily cheated him."

Stated American author Brig. Gen. Telford Taylor (no relation) in his superb work *Münich: The Price of Peace* in 1979:

"Adolf Hitler—busy in Berlin during the entries into Zones 1 and 2—arrived in Hof on the morning of Oct. 3rd and crossed the border at Wildenau, a few miles south of Asch in Zone 3, where he was met by Gen. Guderian...The *Führer* and his entourage drove through Asch toward Eger, stopping for a field kitchen meal alfresco with Reichenau, Guderian, Keitel, Himmler, Henlein, and other dignitaries. Unhappily, there was meat in the stew; the vegetarian dictator munched apples and requested a change in the menu for the remainder of his visit.

"Hitler traveled through the Sudetenland under the protection of an escort commanded by the then little-known Col. Erwin Rommel...After an enthusiastic reception in Eger, he returned to Hof for the night, and the next day visited Karlsbad...Bloodless conquest and pretty girls throwing flowers and bestowing kisses induced a general euphoria and expansiveness among the troops at all levels of rank."

The same Hitler-Rommel duo invaded the rest of "Czechia," as Hitler contemptuously called what was left of rump Czechoslovakia, on March 15, 1939, the Ides of March. Recalled Irving:

"At 2:03 PM, Hitler's train reached the little Bohemian station of Leipa, where the *panzer/armored* corps commander Gen. Erich Hoeppner awaited him with Col. Erwin Rommel (who was to command the *FHQ,* as he had in October 1938).

"To the consternation of Himmler and the security staff, Hitler decided to drive at once to Prague in person, and Hoeppner said he would vouch for the *Führer's* safety. Rommel agreed, and Hitler announced: 'I'm going in!'

"At 4 PM, the frontier barrier was raised for Hitler to cross into Czechoslovakia, and in a driving snowstorm his truck convoy headed on to Prague. It was dusk when they arrived. The roads were choked with *Wehrmacht* transport and troops, and treacherous with ice; one of the trucks of Hitler's convoy rolled over into a ditch. He stood in his open car, returning the salute as he passed his regiments...

"Nobody knew where (Czech President Dr. Emil) Hacha's official residence, the Hradcany Castle, was at first. Hitler's drivers finally entered it through a gate in the rear. The grounds were blanketed in a dazzling snow; German troops milled around in the confusion and darkness. A palace flunkey was found to guide them to a wing where these unexpected visitors might sleep, but even so, Hitler's adjutants had to sleep on the floor...."

Hitler left Prague the next day, never to return.

British author Desmond Young embellished on this incident in his excellent 1950 work *Rommel*:

"When the Germans were about to enter Prague…Rommel was again in command of the escort battalion. 'What would you do if you were in my place, colonel?' the *Führer* asked him. Rommel's answer was in character, 'I should get into an open car,' he said, 'and drive through the street to the *Hradschin/Hradcany* without an escort.'

"With the Czechs in the mood they were in, this was advice which few men, personally responsible for Hitler's safety, would have offered. It was also advice which few men in Hitler's position would have taken, but he took it, and the old newsreels show them acting upon Hitler's suggestion."

The following May, Hitler and his G-4 Gray Column inspected Dr. Todt's *West Wall/ Siegfried Line* opposite the French *Maginot Line*, as he'd done in August 1938, according to Gen. Taylor. During the prior tour:

"The inspection began at the northern end of the fortifications near Aachen, where (Gen. Wilhelm) Adam met the party on the morning of Aug. 27, 1938, and ended three days later at the Swiss border.

"This was Adam's first opportunity to speak with Hitler since Aug. 4th, when Adam had promised Brauchitsch to tell Hitler the true facts about the western defense situation. Once he found himself inside Hitler's car, the blunt old Bavarian lost no time in bringing matters to issue, in a direct and peremptory matter.

"The conference compartment was crowded, with insufficient room to spread the maps, and Adam began by declaring that his briefing was for the *Führer* and his military advisors, and that the civilians—including Himmler, (Labor Service Chief Konstantin) Hierl, and Todt—should leave.

"Despite a few sneers, Adam carried his point (though the three just named—unbeknownst to Adam—crept back into the compartment later), but Hitler was put in a bad humor from the start."

After Gen. Adam noted that the construction wouldn't be finished on schedule, he added that the Western Powers might indeed attack before they were ready:

"This last remark was too much for the *Führer*. 'We have no time to listen to this stuff,' he shouted, 'You understand nothing! The English have no army reserves. The French are internally embroiled.'

"…The party set off in automobiles, Adam in the lead car with the officer who knew the route, Hitler in the second car with the commander of the unit to be visited, and the others bringing up the rear—an order which Adam stuck to throughout the tour. They drove through the Eifel, the hilly, wooded lands between the Rhine (River) and the Low Countries, stopping at various points for briefings by Adam and the unit commanders…

"As in the case of the (earlier) Göring tour, there were large popular demonstrations along the way, and Adam thought much of it spontaneous…Toward the end of the first day, the group reached Saarbrucken…On the second day, the tour passed through the Rheinpfalz to Buhl in southern Baden…

"On the third day, the group continued up the east bank of the Rhine and to the Swiss border…Bidding (area commander-in-chief) Adam goodbye, Hitler professed as his only regret 'That I am the *Führer* and Reich Chancellor, and not the C-in-C of the Western Front.' To others, he declared that 'The man who could not hold these fortifications is a scoundrel!'"

Here is Heinrich Hoffmann's account of the 1939 jaunt into Prague, from *Hitler was my Friend*:

"On March 14th, I was dining with Hitler. 'It was exactly a year ago today,' I remarked, 'that we marched into Vienna.…Only a very few months later came the Sudetenland.' Hitler gave me a quick look, 'And more to come yet…'

"At the (Czech) frontier itself, we were met by a fleet of armored half-tracked (sic) Mercedes cars, in which we continued our onward journey, and on the evening of March 15, 1939—in the middle of a severe snowstorm—we entered Prague, unrecognized and unobserved.

"Hitler's arrival came as a complete surprise, and in view of the secrecy which had surrounded it, no precautions had been made. We drove straight up to the *Hradschin*—the famous Prague fortress—where we took up our quarters.…"

Out of this experience came Hoffmann's photo book, *With Hitler in Bohemia and Moravia*, like the previous edition, *With Hitler in His Homeland.*

Writing in *Hitler's Personal Security*, Dr. Peter Hoffmann made the following interesting notations of the entry into the Sudetenland:

"Hitler began to inspect his new acquisitions on Oct. 3, 1938. He crossed the former border at Wildenau near Asch, in his familiar three-axle Mercedes G-4, having taken his *Führersonderzug/Leader Special Train* from Berlin to Hof on Oct. 2nd.

"He motored from Hof to Asch, Eger, and back to Hof via Wildstein and Schonbach. On Oct. 4th, he traveled via Falkenau and Karlsbad to Annaberg, and then returned to Berlin to open the Winter Aid Program (*Winterhilfe*) campaign for 1938-39 on Oct. 5th. He left Berlin again on the same day for Lobau in Saxony.

"On Oct. 6th, he continued his inspection of the Sudetenland, visiting Fugau, Schluckenau, Rumburg, Kratzau, Friedland, and some formerly Czech fortifications by car, and traveling on by train during the night. On Oct. 7th, he appeared in Neustadt in Upper Silesia, Schonwiese, Kohlbach, Jagerndorf, at some more Czech bunkers, and at Freudenthal.…

"When Hitler passed through the various towns along his route, German troops had taken over the territory only two or three days before, in the first few instances. Cordoning off the streets through which the cars of Hitler's party traveled was often inadequate, and at times, haphazard…There were stretches of crowded streets where cordoning-off troops were not present at all.

"On many occasions, the crowds were not controlled and flooded the street, and they mobbed Hitler's car so that it could not move at all, or only at a snail's pace. Then the *FBK* men had to get out and walk or trot alongside Hitler's Mercedes, three on each side, to try and put at least the distance of their own widths between the crowds and the car. The situation could get quite touchy; the faces of the bodyguards and even of Hitler himself—standing up in his car and presumably enjoying the ovations—showed concern and anger at times.

"On one occasion, in Krumau, a large, framed painting was handed up into the *Führer's* car by someone who wished to express his gratitude—this could easily have been a disguised bomb. Hitler also accepted many bunches of flowers, and even a basket of fruit.

"In another town, one of the strings of little flags hung across the street at the third-story level was dropped down in front of Hitler's car windscreen, whether on purpose or by accident is not clear.

"If it had been strong cord or wire, it could have prevented the car from proceeding for a few critical moments, and the possibility of this as part of an assassination plot could not be excluded.

"In Schluckenau, on Oct. 6th, Hitler reviewed the Sudeten German Free Corps... Flowers by the thousand were thrown in Eger and in Franzenbad..."

Next came the entry into Prague on the Ides of March 1939:

"On the night of March 15-16, Hitler got on his *Führersonderzug* and traveled south, as far as the border town of Bohmisch-Leipa, where he arrived at 3 PM on March 16th.... He continued his trip in his customary three-axle Mercedes to Prague, where he arrived in the evening, held conferences with commanding generals in the *Hradschin* Palace, and then returned to the *Führersonderzug,* where he spent the night.

"...Although Hitler faced an entirely new situation now—traveling in a country that definitely had not wished to be annexed—he still rode his open tourer through the streets of Prague and other towns. The crowds were apparently controlled more easily than in the Sudeten areas, but much of this control was self-control imposed by hostility.

"Hardly anyone seemed to have felt a desire to rush up to Hitler's car and give him flowers, and flowers were not thrown in his path here. The photographs taken by the Reich Photo Reporter and his crew show no instances of flower-giving or flower-tossing, and only once or twice is anyone seen rushing up to Hitler's car.

"In Prague, there were, of course, a certain numbers of supporters of German occupation, among a total German-speaking population (many of them Jews) of some 40,000....Remarkably, few of the onlookers smiled or waved, and Hitler took it in, sitting down most of the time. Only when he met a German Army column did he stand up occasionally and salute. His car was open, but all the windows (bullet-proof glass) were up.

"His car was preceded by two *Führer* Escort cars (open tourers) and then by two armored cars, and followed by the cars of the suite and some more *FBK*. On March 17th in Bratislava—to which he made a detour—the reception was considerably more friendly, and more populace were on hand than in Prague, but security was still tight.

"Many of the preparations for the journeys up to this time had been made *ad hoc* and often at very short notice. By January 1939, a schema was set up of what preparations must be made in what order, and who had to be informed of a forthcoming journey. First of all, in every case, those responsible for all three alternative forms of travel" (car, air, or rail) "had to be informed...Chief driver Kempka had to be told, and it had to be decided whether open or closed cars were needed. In this way, Hitler was always able to make his decision as to the mode of travel at the very last moment."

On Oct. 1, 1938, German Army troops began peacefully occupying the ceded areas of the former Czech Sudetenland to Nazi Germany, and Hitler made his entry two days later on 3 October, as seen here at Wildenau, just south of Asch, at the western tip of Bohemia, in G-4 license plate WH-32288. In this photo Hitler's car approaches the frontier barrier, which is down, as Reich Photo Reporter Prof. Heinrich Hoffmann (left) rushes forward on Hitler's side of the barrier to get a historic "snap" with his Leica camera. The *Führer* is seen giving the Nazi salute standing up in the front passenger seat of the car. (HHA, USNA, College Park, MD/USA.)

A panoramic close up of the very same scene, this time with the Wildenau sign barrier being raised at right to allow a joyous Hitler in G-4 WH-32288 to enter, Oct. 3, 1938. German Sudetenland Nazi leader Konrad Henlein walks at left next to the car's fender, while at right is RSD commander *Standartenfuhrer* Johann Rattenhuber. In the rear of the car at center—just above the windshield—can be seen *SS Führer* aide Gen. Julius Schaub. (HHA, USNA, College Park, MD/USA.)

Two more close-up views of the same scene and event. Hitler stands in the car as Kempka drives. Outside the vehicle, on the far right is RSD commander *Standartenfuhrer* Johann Rattenhuber. (HHA, USNA, College Park, MD/USA.)

The very same car at the Nevada State Penitentiary outside Las Vegas, NV/USA, in 2000, where it was refurbished.The vehicle was then in the Imperial Palace Casino and Automobile Collection, the curator of which was Richie Clyne. Sitting in the car here is author Blaine Taylor. Note also the second G-4 with hood up at left. (Previously-unpublished photo by Dave Hoshall, IPCAC.)

According to the popular British magazine *After the Battle* in its November 2005 edition, "In the winter of 2000, Blaine (Taylor) stood in the very same car in the exact spot Hitler did, in the Nevada State Penitentiary, where the collection of cars owned by the late Ralph Louis Engelstad was worked on by inmates in a special arrangement with the Governor of that State. Upon release, the prisoners were able to get jobs with the Imperial Palace Casino and Museum where some of the other cars were housed in Las Vegas until Engelstad's death in November 2002. After this picture was taken, Blaine was given a tour of a museum adjacent to the owner's Las Vegas suburban home where he personally saw and counted a full 57 other Hitler cars! Following the owner's death—according to still resident director of the Museum Richie Clyne—the entire collection was dispersed by the attorneys of the late owner, with no further information to be made available at their order due to the controversial nature of these vehicles even to this day.They are believed to be in the hands of private collectors around the world at this time." (D. Hoshaw.)

This page and following: Five separate views of the *Führer's* G-4 license plate WH-32288 entering the Sudeten German town of *Karlovy Vary* (*Karlsbad*) on Oct. 4, 1938, following that of Asch and Eger the day before, with *SS* chauffeur Erich Kempka driving. Seated in the car also and seen in the second shot in steel helmet is Army Gen. Walther von Reichenau. The *SSBK* man walking beside the car at lower left in the fourth photo is Bruno Gesche, who was cross-eyed, leading Hitler to joke, "Don't let Gesche sit behind me—he might shoot me in the back by mistake!" As in Berlin on July 6, 1940, the streets of Karlsbad are strewn with flowers, leading Germans later to call the occupations of Austria and the Sudetenland the *Blumenkrieg* (*Flower Wars*). (HHA, USNA, College Park, MD/USA.)

HOTEL ZUR POST

The *Führer* enters Jagerndorf, in the Sudetenland, on Oct. 8, 1938, in G-4 license plate WH-32288. Hitler and chauffeur Erich Kempka ride in front. Hitler's military adjutant Maj. Rudolf Schmundt is on the left mid-car jump seat, and *SS* guard Karl Wilhelm Krause rides on the left rear seat. (HHA, USNA, College Park, MD/USA.)

Hitler enters Freudenthal, in the Sudetenland, on Oct. 7, 1938, in G-4 license plate WH-32288 as he receives a delirious reception. Hitler and *SS* driver Erich Kempka are in front. Maj. Rudolf Schmundt (left) and *SS Führer* valet Heinz Linge (right) are on the jump seats in the middle of the vehicle. *SS* bodyguard Karl Wilhelm Krause (left), *SS* Gen. Julius Schaub (center), and *SS* adjutant Max Wünsche (right) are in the rear seating section. Stated one eyewitness of the Sudeten entry, recalling it in 1973, "We lived in a Czech border village. They were already building bunkers there, the Czechs. It was a relief when the Germans marched into the Sudetenland—a liberation. 'It can only get better,' people said at the time. Hitler drove through, too, standing up in the car without holding onto anything. It was fascinating, like mass hypnosis. The Communists were cheering loudly, too! We were all happy," recalled this teacher. *SSBK* officer Bruno Gesche strides at the left of the car. (Previously-unpublished photo from the Hermann Göring Albums, LC, Wash., DC.)

Above and following: A quintet of views of the *Führer's* entry into Eger on Oct. 3, 1938, in G-4 WH-32292. The occupants of the car are Hitler and *SS* driver Erich Kempka up front; Maj. Rudolf Schmundt (left) and *SS* Hitler valet Heinz Linge (right) in the mid-car section; and *SS* bodyguard Karl Wilhelm Krause sitting at left rear. (HHA, USNA, College Park, MD/USA.)

Hitler's triumphant arrival at Freudenthal, in the Sudetenland, on Oct. 7, 1938, in his G-4 with *SSBK* man Bruno Gesche (left) preparing to open his car door so that the *Führer* can step down. At far left—waiting with his informal swagger stick field marshal's baton in hand—is *Luftwaffe* chief Hermann Göring. The SP on the banner at the far right stands for Sudeten Party, the domestic Nazi Party in the Sudetenland. (Previously-unpublished photo by Helmuth Kurth, HGA, LC, Wash., DC.)

20

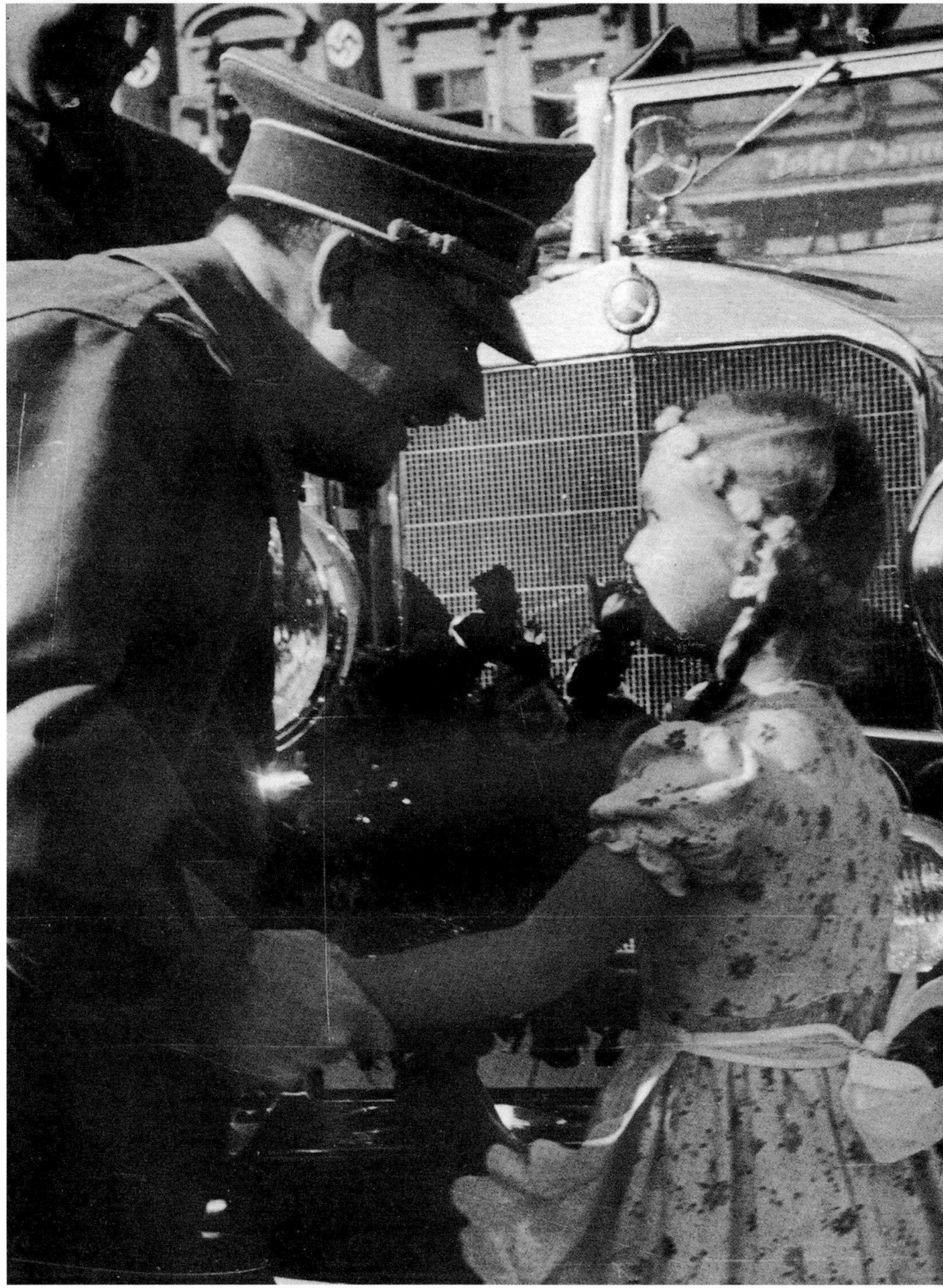

The *Führer* receives welcoming bouquets of flowers from little girls in the town square of Eger, in the Sudetenland, Oct. 3, 1938. In the second scene, note the G-4's famous honeycombed radiator, with the Daimler-Benz corporate logo atop that, and the more famous encircled, three-pointed star overall. (HHA, USNA, College Park, MD/USA.)

As I noted in the December 2007 issue of *Military Illustrated* of this photograph, "'Czechoslovakia's salute to the German Army as it marched across the Czech frontier on Oct. 1, 1938, as published numerous times before, in several cases, this photo has been used as proof that the residents were opposed to Hitler's entry into their homeland, and thus saluting under emotional duress, but the question arises: Are these tears of sorrow or of joy? In *Soldat*, Lt. Knappe testified that he told his friends back in Germany that he saw no Czech soldiers during the entirely peaceful *Blumenkrieg/Flower War* German occupation." Actually, only the *right-hand side* of this historic photo is usually published, as opposed to the full frame seen here. (USNA.)

A German Army *panzer* commander (left) rendering Hitler a military salute. The former wears black jacket and beret. Hitler returns his greeting with a casual, backhanded Nazi salute. In the back left is *SS Führer* adjutant Gen. Julius Schaub, with *SS* bodyguard Karl Wilhelm Krause at center. (HHA, USNA, College Park, MD/USA.)

The *Führer* reviews *SS-Totenkopfestandarte Oberbayern* (*Death's Head Standard-1 Upper Bavaria*) sometime after Oct. 10, 1938, from G-4 license plate WH-32288 in a field in the occupied Sudetenland, as their commander—*SS* Gen. Theodor "Papa" Eicke—stands on the car's running board. *RFSS* Heinrich Himmler stands in the jump seat section at mid-car behind Hitler. (Ulric of England and HHA, USNA, College Park, MD/USNA.)

As I wrote in the December 2007 issue of *Military Illustrated*, "The *Führer's* motorcade makes a roadside stop to inspect a damaged Czech roadblock, Oct. 3, 1938. Hitler in center, with SS bodyguard Karl Wilhelm Krause seen over his shoulder; Hitler's Army adjutant Maj. Rudolf Schmundt stands at right with a map under his left arm, while Gen. Wilhelm Keitel prepares to alight from the *Führer's* G-4 car at far right. The second vehicle is also a Mercedes G-4." (HHA, USNA, College Park, MD/USA.)

Right: The *Führer's* G-4 license plate WH-37925 passes by drawn up German Army soldiers in just-occupied Prague on the afternoon of March 16, 1939. (HHA, USNA, College Park, MD/USA.)

The *Führer* salutes from G-4 license plate WH-37925 in Prague, reviewing his troops after he arrived there on March 16, 1939. Note that the much-reported "blinding snowstorm" of the night before has faded completely away! Note also the horse-drawn caissons of the famous "mechanized" German Army of 1939—largely the same way in 1945 as well! (HHA, USNA, College Park, MD/USA.)

The *Führer's* G-4 license plate WH-37925 in Prague on March 16, 1939, with the armored cars of his military escort riding ahead. Again, no snow is visible anywhere from the night before. The scene is eerily familiar, however, for another reason as well, resembling as it does the streetcar site of *SS* Gen. Reinhard Heydrich's roadside assassination of 1942! (HHA, USNA, College Park, MD/USA.)

A pair of views of Hitler's G-4 license plate WH-37925 entering Brunn, Czechoslovakia, on March 16, 1939. The passengers are the *Führer* and *SS* driver Erich Kempka up front, Maj. Rudolf Schmundt on the left middle jump seat and, behind him on the rear seat, *SS* bodyguard Karl Wilhelm Krause. Noted English author Andrew Mollo in *The Pictorial History of the SS 1923-45*, "Hitler sped through the streets of Brunn and on to Prague, where he spent the night at the Hradschin Castle, the ancient seat of the Kings of Bohemia, overlooking the River Moldau." (HHA, USNA, College Park, MD/USA.)

A pair of views of the *Führer's* G-4 license plate WH-37925 as he enters Prague on March 16, 1939. Note that the vehicle's snow chains are on the spare tires, and that the front bulletproof windows only are rolled up as he stands to salute. (HHA, USNA, College Park, MD/USA.)

Started in 1937, the Nazi *West Wall* (*Siegfried Line*) was originally scheduled for completion 20 years hence, or by 1957, but Hitler ordered construction speeded up to intimidate Britain and France. He believed that the stratagem worked, making the Allies cave in at the Münich Conference of Sept. 29-30, 1938, over his territorial demands for the Czech-German Sudetenland, as he told Gen. Wilhelm Keitel. As the later Polish Crisis of 1939 loomed, the *Führer* once more placed emphasis on the *West Wall* fortifications between Nazi Germany and Republican France, and took much publicized tours in both years, in August 1938 and May 1939, in G-4 cross-country open touring cars. Here—during the May 1939 tour—Hitler (in rarely worn white raincoat) examines a bunker, as Martin Bormann stands behind him. On the roadway in the distance stands the *Führer Kolonne* (*Leader Column*) of a line of over a dozen field gray painted G-4s. (HHA, USNA, College Park, MD/USA.)

One of this author's favorite G-4 shots: Hitler entering Prague on March 16, 1939, in license plate WH-37925. Note the *Führerstandarte* at left, the rolled up leather engine radiator cover at center, and the spare tires on both sides of the car with winter snow chains in place, but *not*—interestingly!—on the tires meeting the road. Two *SS* Hitler security men walk beside the vehicle at the left. (HHA, USNA, College Park, MD/USA.)

During the May 1939 tour of the *West Wall*, Hitler explains his plans to his entourage, with a pair of G-4s seen at right rear. Behind the *Führer* stands his *Luftwaffe* liaison officer, Maj. Nikolaus von Below. To the left of von Below is Martin Bormann, and to the left of him is the man responsible for the building of the fortifications, engineer Dr. Fritz Todt, looking down at the map table. (HHA, USNA, College Park, MD/USA.)

A map table briefing during the May 1939 G-4 *West Wall* tour. From left to right are seen Gen. Erwin von Witzleben (red facings on overcoat), unknown group of aides, Gen. Wilhelm Keitel (hands behind his back), *SS* officer, *RFSS* Heinrich Himmler (hands clasped in front), *Reichsleiter* (*National Leader*) Martin Bormann, unidentified Army officer, *FBK* man Bruno Gesche, Dr. Fritz Todt (leather coat and coffee can cap), and Hitler. (Hugo Jager Collection.)

4

The Polish Campaign September-October 1939

The German invasion of Poland began at 4:45 AM on Sept. 1, 1939, when the Navy battleship *Schleswig-Holstein* opened fire on the Polish fortress garrison of Westerplatte, at the Free City of Danzig, as part of Hitler's *Case White* scenario. The next day, German advances from East Prussia forced the Polish Modlin Army to retreat to its Vistula River line, and on the 3rd, Great Britain and the third French Republic declared war on Nazi Germany. Thus, the Second World War began.

According to writer Justin Tonna in his article *Sabres and Tanks* in the September 2007 issue of *Military Illustrated* magazine:

"Germany's plan to invade Poland involved a three-pronged attack that would take advantage of the long borders shared by the two nations.

"The main attack would come from Army Group South, commanded by Gen. (Gerd) von Rundstedt, which would come through Poland's western borders. A second attack by Army Group North would come through North Prussia, and was under the command of Gen. (Fedor) von Bock. A third assault would come across the Slovakian border by allied Slovakian troops.

"Finally, there were also *Seibstschutz* operating in Poland that would mobilize the German minority to conduct resistance and sabotage operations on the Polish forces...

"Germany invaded Poland with 1.6 million men, 4,000 tanks and 2,000 aircraft. The Poles mustered around 39 divisions and 16 brigades amounting to around 800,000 men, along with approximately 800 armored vehicles and 400 aircraft to defend their homeland...."

Piotkrow fell on the 5th, thus opening the road to Warsaw for the German *panzer* divisions. That same evening, the Polish Lodz, Krakow, Prusy, and Poznan Armies all withdrew behind the Vistula River. By the 7th, the first German tanks reached Warsaw, but were held off by fierce street fighting, a dim preview of later events at Stalingrad during 1942-43.

On the 9th, the German 8th Army was blindsided by a surprise counterattack launched by the Polish Poznan Army. By the 15th, German Army Group North reached the outskirts of Warsaw, thus resuming the delayed siege of the Polish capital. The next day, a massive ground artillery and aerial assault began against Polish forces aligned along the Bzura River, with the retreat to Warsaw beginning that night.

On the 17th—under the terms of the Nazi-Soviet Non-Aggression Pact signed in Moscow the previous 23 August—the Red Army began its invasion of Poland from the east. Two days later, the Polish Krakow Army began its breakout towards neutral Rumania through Tomaszow Lubelski, and on the 21st, the last Polish Army units on the Bzura River line surrendered. Defeated at home, the Poles fought on in other theaters until 1945.

Encircled by both German and Soviet forces, the Polish city of Lvov surrendered on the 22nd. Three days later, the *Luftwaffe* launched a massive aerial bombardment of Warsaw, the first such of World War II, and on the 26th, the southern Warsaw forts fell, with the entire garrison surrendering on the 28th. The Polish Army Modlin garrison fell on the 29th, and on 5 October the Nazi *Führer* reviewed his sole victory parade of a foreign capital in Warsaw. The Poles put a German *panzer* division out of action in numbers.

The first German *blitzkrieg* campaign ended on October 6, 1939, when the Polish Army Battlegroup under Gen. Franciszek Kleeberg surrendered following a four-day struggle around Kock, Poland. The Germans lost 40,000 casualties in six weeks.

Concluded writer Tonna:

"The Polish campaign cost the Germans 16,000 men, enough equipment for an entire armored division, and a substantial amount of its air strength. The campaign lasted approximately one week less than the conquest of France—and France was considered to correspond much closer to Germany in terms of equipment and troop numbers."

The Poles suffered 200,000 killed and wounded overall.

As to Hitler's own, personal schedule throughout the unprecedentedly swift Polish campaign, we turn to author Aaron L. Johnson's superb 1999 work, *Hitler's Military Headquarters: Organization, Structures, Security, and Personnel.* From 3-19 September, the *Führer* resided in his first wartime military *FHQ*, Special Train *Amerika* (after 1943 codenamed *Brandenburg*), and from then through the 25th at the Hotel Casino at Zoppot, Danzig, Poland.

On 26 September Hitler returned to Berlin by train, and on 5 October flew from there to Warsaw, landing at *O Kecie* airfield outside the city at 11:30 AM, and reviewed the victory parade of the German Army and *Waffen SS* the same day.

Johnson also provides the following schedule:

"Sept. 4th, Kulm and the Polish Corridor area; 5th, Polish Corridor area; 6th, Tuchler Heath; 7th-10th, PC area; 11th, Lodz and Rava areas; 13th, Lodz; 14th, PC; 15th, Galicia (Jaroslav and Ubieszyn); 16th-18th, Galicia and PC area; 19th, Oliva, Zoppot, and Danzig; 20th, Zoppot; 21st, Westerplatte, Gdingen, and Oxhoft; 22nd, Praga/Warsaw, Zoppot; 23rd-24th, Zoppot; 25th, Zoppot, Bzura area; Oct. 5th, Warsaw."

During Hitler's time on Special Train *Amerika* and at Zoppot, he made almost daily Mercedes-Benz G-4 road trips to the front to visit his troops in the Gray Column of the wartime *Führer Kolonne*, again—for the third and last time—under the personal command of now Gen. Rommel.

Added Prof. Peter Hoffmann in *Hitler's Personal Security*:

"Two motor convoys were directed wherever the *Führersonderzug/Leader Special Train* went, to be available at a moment's notice for a drive…At 9:30 AM (on Sept. 4th), the *Führer's* motor convoy left for the first tour of the front area.

"All cars were open Mercedes, still in glossy beige with black mudguards, but with license plates and other insignia covered (by the time of the French campaign, the cars would be painted dull-olive gray).

"Two groups were formed. In the first group there were Hitler's car, two *Führer-Begleit-Kommando/Security* cars, a car for the aides, and a car for the Chief of OKW (Keitel), and some more aides. In Hitler's car, there were—besides the *Führer* (who now carried a gun on his belt)—and the driver (Kempka), Schaub, Schmundt, Capt. von Below, Capt. (Gerhard) Engel, and Linge (with a machine-pistol).

"The next two cars carried *FBK* men and Brückner, with two machine guns each mounted on several of the open cars. Usually the *SS Escort* car followed immediately behind Hitler's car, and the *RSD* car was next.

"In the adjutants' car sat Martin Bormann, Maj. Gen. (Karl) Bodenschatz, an SS aide of lower rank, and the Reich Photo Reporter (Heinrich Hoffmann.) In the fifth car there were Gen. (Later Field Marshal) Keitel and one of his adjutants, the liaison officers of the Army and Navy, and one of the Air Force.

"The second convoy consisted of two 'Ministers' cars, with (Foreign Minister Joachim von) Ribbentrop and (Reich Chancellery Chief Dr. Hans Heinrich) Lammers and their aides, one car for Himmler and his aides and bodyguards, one for Reich Press Chief Dr. (Otto) Dietrich, one for other persons invited to accompany the *Führer*, a reserve car, a field kitchen car, and a petrol tanker.

"The two groups of cars—already well-armed—were surrounded by a *Frontgruppe/Front Group* of the evolving *FBK* under Rommel's command. Hitler's group was preceded by a squad of five soldiers on motorcycles and by two armed reconnaissance vehicles, and five more motorcycle soldiers brought up the rear, followed immediately by the Headquarters Commandant's (Rommel's) car, five more motorcycle soldiers, a signal corps platoon, and an anti-aircraft platoon with their guns.

"This intermediate column was called Column K (for *Kommandant*). It was followed at an interval of five minutes by elements protecting Group 2, known as Column M (apparently for military). They consisted of an anti-tank gun, followed by the cars of Group 2, after which there followed another anti-tank gun and parts of the signals platoon accompanying Group 1.

"The first visit to the front in this convoy took the *Führer* and his party as far as the Vistula (River), where German troops were crossing at Topolno, and then back to a new location of the *Führersonderzug*. The journey took the convoy through Neustettin, Preussich Friedland, Zempelburg, and Komierwo, where Hitler was briefed about the situation by Gen. (Hans-Gunther) von Kluge, Commander-in-Chief 4th Army.

"…After lunch from the field kitchen, the party left for Topolno. At one point, the convoy was stopped because only minutes ago some Polish soldiers had ambushed a field hospital company, but when there were no further signs of the Poles, the journey continued.

"About eight kilometers from Crone, an oncoming lorry collided with one of the vehicles of the anti-aircraft platoon, but none of the drivers was at fault. The lorry driver had been shot through the chest by a Polish sniper just as he was going past the *Führer's* convoy.

"As the travelers pressed on through Crone and Brzezno to Pruszcz, the *FieselerStorch/Stork* aircraft that had followed them to provide aerial reconnaissance was shot at by mistake by German troops. Hitler watched the German troops crossing the Vistula (River) at Topolno, and returned to Topolno to inspect some unfinished Polish bunkers.

"While he was there, Polish planes began dropping bombs only two or three kilometers away, whereupon the convoy began its retreat through Vandsburg and Flatow to Plienitz…

"The next trip to the front—on Sept. 6th from Gross-Born…to Plewno where Gen. Guderian commanded XIX Army Corps, and on to the Vistula bridge at Graudenz, was less eventful, as were the ones on Sept. 10, 11, 13, and 15th. On Sept. 10th…a motor convoy had been sent ahead to Bialaczow from where the party drove to Konskie and to Maslow. Security was lax…

"Hitler was still shaking hands as they gradually cleared a lane for his Mercedes G-4. Similar mob scenes occurred at many stops. In towns, and even on the highway, the column often moved at a snail's pace along narrow streets and dusty roads congested with horse-drawn wagons and lorries full of prisoners-of-war going in the opposite direction… Almost every day during his visits to the Polish Front—and in every conceivable manner—Hitler got himself into situations in which his life was in great danger.

"The planes had been flown to Maslow and the group flew back from here to Neudorf and arrived at 6:15 PM by car in Ilnau, where the *Führersonderzug* and Ribbentrop's special train were stationed. On Sept. 11th, an almost identical journey was made to Boguslawice, west of Tomaszow, again by plane, and by car to Wola and back to Ilnau.

"On Sept. 12th, the Special was moved to Gogolin, and another visit to the front followed, partly by air and partly by car. This time Gen. von Blaskowitz southwest of Lodz, Gen. Ulex north of Lodz, and Gen. von Weichs at Bratoszewice had to brief their Supreme Warlord.

"The pace proved too much for the motor convoy. When on Sept. 15th the *Führer's* party arrived in Pawlosiow at 10 AM by plane, there was no convoy there. It finally limped in at 11 AM, after a 22-hour drive, and after several vehicles had broken down.

Hitler could not wait, and a makeshift convoy had been assembled for a look at troops crossing the San River, but when the convoy arrived, it was immediately put into service, and then sent on to Krakow the same afternoon. There it was to be ready for another trip on Sept. 16th, but this was postponed to Sept. 17th, and finally cancelled...

"For Sept. 19th, two alternative plans were prepared: the *Führer* was to choose one of them shortly before departure time...Neither plan was followed in every detail; the first plan—a trip to Danzig—was adopted with modifications.

"The military escort came only as far as Zoppot, the border town, where *Gauleiter/Regional Leader* (Albert) Forster greeted Hitler and his party. Flowers were thrown—the streets were nearly covered with them in places—and great crowds filled the pavements and the windows and balconies...

"A trip to Westerplatte by minesweeper, and from here by motor convoy via Zoppot to Gdingen—which was scheduled for Sept. 19th—a trip to Dirschau to see a blown up bridge planned for Sept. 20th was moved to Sept. 22nd. On this day, the *Führer* observed the artillery bombardment of Praga, a suburb of Warsaw, and then went by car to Wyszkow...

"His next trip to Poland...took him to Warsaw by plane on Oct. 5th for the great victory parade. He was met at the airport by his victorious generals, Brauchitsch, Milch, Rundstedt, Blaskowicz, and Cochenhausen, and was escorted by an Army detachment into Warsaw to the parade ground opposite the Dutch Embassy. The parade lasted for two and a half hours."

According to the unpublished manuscript placed at this author's disposal by the late *FHQ* expert and author Dr. Richard Raiber of Hockessin, DE (*Führer-Begleit-Batallion*):

"The *Kommandant* (Rommel) had been informed that Hitler intended to make tours of the front by motor convoy, for which adequate military protection would be required...Gen. Rommel had organized a motorized Front Group from his battalion for this mission.

"In the event, Hitler would make eight tours of the front in Poland in September 1939.

"Several years before the war began, a series of Mercedes-Benz vehicles—770G4W31s, and called G-4s—had been developed to be at Hitler's disposal when he traveled outside of Germany. Heavy, three-axle, cross-country automobiles with three bench-type seats and canvas folding tops, G-4s...advanced, armored models were available for Hitler's tours of the front in September 1939.

"On each, two 7.92mm machine guns (MG 34s, later replaced by MG 42s) were mounted on pintles. They were always driven by SS officers or NCOs belonging to the *SS-Begleitkommando*.

"Although the terminology tended to vary slightly, a cavalcade of G-4s transporting Hitler was often called a *Führer Column/Führerkolonne*. When the latter was escorted by a Front Group, the convoy might be known as a *Front Column/Frontkolonne*....

"On Aug. 31, 1939, Gen. Rommel organized a Front Group to protect the *Führer's* tour of the front...as follows: There were three divisions. Escort Column F included five motorcyclists at the point, followed by two armored reconnaissance vehicles.

"Next came the *Führer* Column: five G-4s, the first carrying Hitler and his close associates, then two for the *FBK* (*SS-Begleitkommando* in number 2, and the *Kriminalkommando* in number 3), another for adjutants, and the fifth for the aides of the officers riding with Hitler.

"Trailing these were two armored reconnaissance vehicles, followed by five motorcyclists bringing up the rear. Escort Column K was made up of the Kommandant's vehicle, five motorcyclists, and then vehicles transporting a signals staff and a flak platoon.

"Escort Column F departed first, followed at once by the *Führer* Column. Column M waited for five minutes after departure of Column K, and then got off. Its vehicles carried the *Führer* of the anti-tank platoon, an anti-tank cannon (Czech PAK), other individuals designated by the *Führer* to participate in the tour of the front, and trucks for baggage, a field mess, a second PAK, and the rest of the signals platoon.

"On Sept. 3, 1939, Col. Rudolf Schmundt—the *Führer's* Chief Armed Forces Adjutant—arranged the order and composition for the next day's tour. There were two groups: Echelon 1 consisted of the *Führer* car—Hitler's G-4—which transported Hitler. *SS* Gen. Julius Schaub (one of Hitler's personal adjutants), Col. Schmundt, Capt. Nikolaus von Below (Hitler's Air Force adjutant), Army adjutant Capt. Gerhard Engel, and a servant.

"Escort car 1—with the *SS-Begleitkommando* component of the *FBK* aboard—was under the direction of Chief Personal Adjutant and SA Lt. Gen. Wilhelm Brückner. Escort car 2—carrying the Criminal Command—was led by *SS* Capt. Peter Högl. In the Adjutant car rode *Reichsleiter* Martin Bormann, Air Force Maj. Gen. Karl Bodenschatz (Hermann Göring's representative at the FHQ), *SS* 1st Lt. Max Wünsche (Hitler's SS adjutant), escort physician *SS* Dr. Karl Brandt, and court photographer Heinrich Hoffmann.

"Next was *OKW/High Command of the Armed Forces* chief Col. Gen. Wilhelm Keitel, an escort, liaison officers Col. Nikolaus von Vormann (Army), and Capt. Klostermann (Air Force.) Echelon 2 contained Minister car 1, with Foreign Minister Joachim von Ribbentrop, and Dr. Hans-Heinrich Lammers, Chief of the Reich Chancellery, and an escort.

"These were followed by a G-4 carrying *RFSS* Heinrich Himmler, another with Reich Press Chief Dr. Otto Dietrich aboard, and a third transporting other individuals designated by Hitler to participate in the tour. Finally, there was a reserve vehicle, and still others for the baggage, field kitchen, and fuel bringing up the rear of Echelon 2.

"Many functionaries from Berlin had found an excuse to visit the *FHQ*, and on Sept. 6th—when Hitler made his second tour of the front—some even managed to attach themselves and go out with it into the Polish Corridor. In order to evade such encumbrances in the future, the decision was made that Hitler and his close associates would fly to a Polish airfield recently overrun by the *Wehrmacht*, convenient to the areas he wished to visit, and tour in a Front Column, which would've met him there.

"At 5:30 PM, Sept. 9, 1939, Front Group Bertram (named for its leader, Capt. Erik Bertram, a *Luftwaffe* officer on Maj. Gen. Rommel's staff), departed from Ilnau, near Oppeln in Silesia—where the *Führersonderzug* was then parked—and drove eastward into Poland.

"It consisted of a command troop, a motorcycle messenger platoon, an armored reconnaissance platoon, a signals staff, a press truck, a Flak platoon, and one-half of a PAK platoon. Empty *SS-Begleitkommando*-driven G-4s—including the *Führer* car—were part of the convoy.

"Early next morning, the Front Group reached its rendezvous point, a captured Polish landing field at Bialaczow, 15 kilometers northwest of Konskie, and 320 kilometers from the *Führersonderzug* at Ilnau. It was waiting when Hitler and the others arrived at 10 AM in a flight of Ju-52s escorted by German fighters. The *Führer* car had been driven by SS 2nd Lt. Schneider, who delivered it to *SS* Maj. Erich Kempka, Hitler's personal driver, who had flown with Hitler in Ju 52 D-AVAU.

"That day, the Front Column took Hitler to the area of operations of the German 10th Army, and, in the afternoon, to a seized Polish airfield at Maslow, 14 kilometers northeast of Kielce, where Hitler held a briefing conference with a group of commanding generals. Meanwhile, the Ju 52s had landed at Maslow, and later in the afternoon, returned Hitler and his associates to the *Führersonderzug*....

"Officers and men of Front Group Bertram—weary from their mission in Poland—were given little rest: early next day, they were sent out again to meet the *Führer's* Ju 52s, this time at the Lodz Municipal Airport, for his tour on Sept. 13th. For the next two weeks, the Front Group remained in the rear areas of Poland, driving from one captured landing field to another as directed by radioed instructions from the *Führersonderzug,* to receive Hitler, and escort his tours of the front.

"When the Ju 52s landed at Palosiow—the airfield serving Jaroslaw in Galicia on Sept. 15th—Hitler found that Front Group Bertram and the G-4s had not yet arrived. A vehicle was commandeered from 10th Army to transport an irritated Hitler into Jaroslaw, where he observed a division cross the San River.

"This was one of the very few occasions in the course of the war when Hitler was not driven in his own *Führer* car by his own chauffeur. He was relieved when an exhausted Front Group Bertram rolled into Jaroslaw at last, so that Maj. Kempka could take over the wheel of the *Führer* car for the remainder of the tour.

"In it, he was driven to the San (River) at Sieniawa, 15 kilometers north of Jaroslaw, where he watched another river crossing before returning to Paloslow. Front Group Bertram had been at Lodz when its marching orders were received, and had pushed for 22 hours without rest on the 300-kilometer, cross-country trek to Jaroslaw. Among other trials and tribulations, it had endured was a broken axle sustained by the *Führer* car, which *Wehrmacht* mechanics—fortunately in the vicinity—had been able to repair.

"On Sept. 22nd, Front Group Bertram escorted Hitler's round trip tour from the landing field at Wyskow, northeast of Warsaw, to Gliniki, where—from a church steeple—Hitler could see artillery shells landing in the Polish capital, 10 miles to the west. On Sept. 25th, the Front Group met his Ju 52s at Guzow, west of Warsaw, and took him to Wiskitki, Davidy, and Stucewice, 12 kilometers south of Warsaw: there, from a tower, Hitler and the others watched a bombardment of Warsaw's southern suburbs.

"On Sept. 26th—with the campaign all but over—Hitler returned in the *Führersonderzug* to Berlin. On the same day, Front Group Bertram drove westward to reach its barracks in the Reich capital. It had marked up approximately 4,000 kilometers in scurrying back and forth across the Polish countryside as it furnished military protection for Hitler's front tours."

Stated British author Gen. Desmond Young in his epochal biography *Rommel: The Desert Fox* in 1950:

"From Hitler's headquarters, Rommel had a bird's-eye view of the lightning campaign which overwhelmed Poland in four weeks, before the bulk of the Polish Army had even reached its concentration areas. On Sept. 2nd, he was at Pruszczo, on the 10th at Kielce, on the 13th at Lodz, and on Oct. 5th at Warsaw, which had capitulated on Sept. 30th. A day or two later, he was on his way back to Berlin."

Added British revisionist historian David Irving in his groundbreaking 1977 study *Hitler's War*:

"At 8 AM on the morning of Sept. 4th...Gen Fedor von Bock—the commander of Army Group North—joined Rommel in reporting to Hitler, and the three men set out on an extended tour of the battle areas.

"Accompanied by his adjutants and a manservant, Hitler rode in a heavy, six-wheeled Mercedes, and the rest of his staff and escort followed in six identical vehicles [G-4s]. The little convoy—headed by two armored scout cars—with two more bringing up the rear, drove off to visit 4th Army headquarters; 70 or more cars packed with Party and Ministerial personages jostled for position behind the *Führer's* convoy, completely ignoring the vehicle sequence orders the frantic Schmundt had drawn up.

"A choking cloud of Pomeranian dust was flung up from the unpaved country roads. At each brief halt, the same undignified scenes were repeated as Hitler's generals and Party leaders elbowed their way into the foreground of the photographs being taken and then galloped back to their cars to urge their chauffeurs into even closer proximity to the *Führer's* Mercedes.

"Once, when Martin Bormann angrily rebuked Rommel for these scenes of disorder, the general coolly snapped back, 'I'm not a kindergarten teacher—*you* sort them out if you want!'

"Hitler affected not to notice all this—no doubt seeing it as further proof of his own popularity. During the first days of the campaign, no way could be found to shake off this horde of idle camp followers, but eventually Schmundt did manage to elude most of them by beginning each visit to the front with a short flight in the three available Junkers 52s to an airfield where a little motor convoy was waiting [i.e., the Bertram Front Group, as we've seen].

"Everywhere Hitler was surrounded by jubilant soldiers who sensed that this was an historic hour...On the sixth, he toured the battlefield at Tucheler Heide, where a powerful Polish corps had been encircled and now desperately struggled to break out. [Apparently convinced that the German tanks were only tinplate dummies, the Polish cavalry attacked with lances couched.]

"Here the roads were littered with the carnage of unequal battle. A radio message told Hitler that Krakow was now in German hands. As he had hoped, the greater part of the Polish Army had been trapped west of the Vistula, while the strong force assembled at Posen for the attack on Berlin was now aimless and isolated—far from the main scene of events…

"Hitler's tours of these battlefields were his first real contact with 'the East.' They reinforced his unhealthy fantasies about the 'sub-humans' and the Jews. On Sept. 10th, he had visited the 10th Army, busy finishing off the Polish forces encircled at Radom….

"Hitler's positive enjoyment of the battle scenes was undeniable. He visited the front whenever he could, heedless to the risk to himself and his escort. It irritated him when his convoy took a wide detour around the city of Lodz en route to 8th Army headquarters, and he ordered that, on the way back, the convoy was to drive right through the heart of the city. (An order the unhappy Army authorities fulfilled by cordoning off the entire route, clearing away the Polish population in neighboring streets and conducting Hitler's convoy at an uninterrupted 50 miles an hour, two vehicles abreast, from one end of the city to the other.)

"He enjoyed meeting his troops and—for all we know—was exhilarated by the smell of cordite and the sight of blood…On the 15th, we find Hitler at Jaroslav, watching his soldiers bridging the river San…

"By Sept. 19th, when Hitler and his staff drove into Danzig, the Polish campaign was all but over….As the victorious *Führer* drove through the streets of Danzig for the first" (and the only) "time, flowers rained down from the windows, swastika flags draped the streets, and the crowds of German Danzigers were wild with emotion.

"When the convoy of cars stopped outside the ancient *Artus Hof,* Schmundt was overheard to comment to a newer staff member, 'It was like this everywhere—in the Rhineland, in Vienna, in the Sudeten territories, and in Memel. Do you still doubt the mission of the *Führer*?'….

"Afterward, his staff cleared a path for him through the heaving Danzig population packed into the Long Market outside."

Thus, the whirlwind German campaign of 1939 in Poland, and the first wartime sorties of his fabled G-4 touring cars!

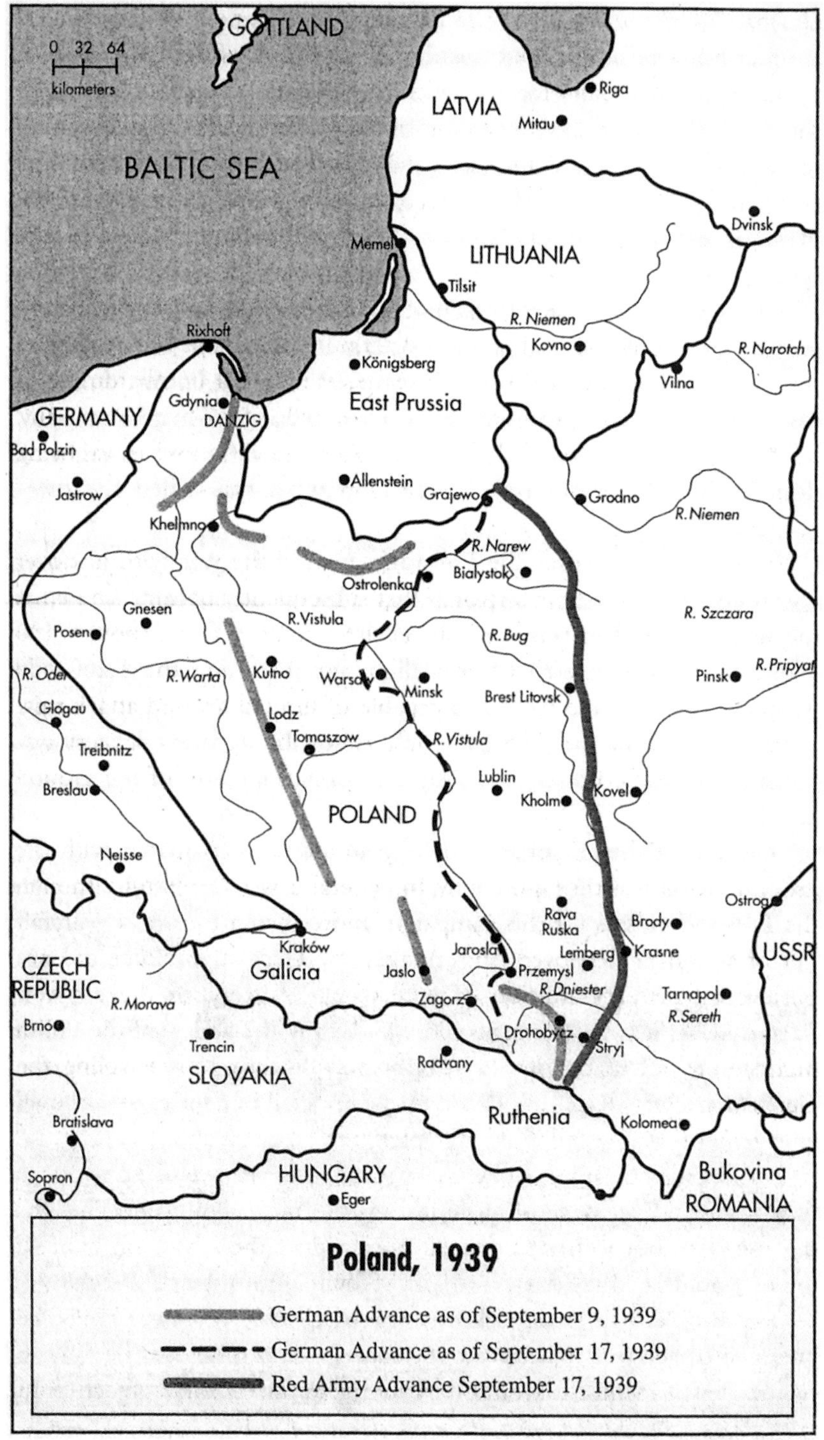

Map of Poland 1939. (From *The Blitzkrieg Myth* by John Mosier, 2003.)

A previously-unpublished view of the *Führersondersug* (*Leader Special Train*) *Amerika* (codenamed *Brandenburg* in 1943) in the background as *Luftwaffe* C-in-C Field Marshal Hermann Göring (left) and *RFSS* Heinrich Himmler (right) are seen at center with a G-4 parked at the far right, above which is Hitler *SS* aide Max Wünsche (right.) Stated German Army Gen. Walter Warlimont—Jodl's deputy at Section L within *FHQ*—in his excellent 1964 study *Inside Hitler's Headquarters 1939-45*, "The *Führer Special* was stationed in the training area of Gross-Born (Pomerania); from this area we went off every other day on tours of the front lasting from early morning until late at night, visiting Army and Corps headquarters. At each place, the *Führer* had the situation presented to him; occasionally, he happened to meet the Commander-in-Chief of the Army (von Brauchitsch)." Gogolin, Poland, on Sept. 14, 1939. (Hermann Göring Albums, LC, Wash., DC.)

Polish Army prisoners-of-war of the Germans wait an uncertain fate, September 1939. (*Signal*, George Peterson National Capital Historic Sales, Springfield, VA/USA.)

A good right-side view of a Hitlerite G-4 cross country touring car, with *Führerstandarte* in place over the left front fender, and reduced light headlamp coverings on as well for wartime usage. Note, too, the plush leather-coated seats and the thickness of the armor-plated doors and bulletproof glass. Continued Gen. Warlimont in his 1964 account, "Hitler very seldom intervened in the conduct of operations; I can myself only think of two instances. Otherwise, he did no more than give his point of view, discuss with the Commander-in-Chief of the Army, and make suggestions. He never committed himself so far as to give an order." (HHA, USNA, College Park, MD/USA.)

A destroyed Polish Army unit in Poland, September 1939. Recalled Reich Photo Reporter Prof. Heinrich Hoffmann in 1955, "For the first time in my life I saw a battlefield. On the Tuchler Heide on both sides of the road for as far as the eye could see, lay a confused mass of broken and abandoned guns, rifles, machine guns, first-aid boxes, cast-off equipment of every sort, and horribly mangled corpses of man and horse, rapidly putrefying in the hot September sun. An appalling stench hung over the whole countryside, and it was a terrible and ghastly sight which I shall never forget and which robbed Guderian's brilliantly conceived and executed plan of all its glamour for me." (Captured Enemy Records, USNA, College Park, MD/USA.)

At 9:30 AM on Sept. 4, 1939, the *Führer* left Special Train *Amerika* for his very first G-4 front visit, from Neustettin to Komierow, where he met with the staff of the German 4th Army (Kempka driving). (HHA, USNA, College Park, MD/USA.)

That very same day at noon, from left to right: Gen. Bodenschatz, Hitler, and Linge have lunch on the Tuchler Heath from the motorcade's field kitchen truck. (HHA, USNA, College Park, MD/USA.)

On Sept. 5, 1939, *Amerika* trundled into Grossborn, from which Hitler conducted more such front tours, as here, passing by a mob of captured Polish Army soldiers (left) of the German 3rd *Panzer* Division. (HHA, USNA, College Park, MD/USA.)

The *Führer* Special Train arrived at Illnau bei Oppeln on Sept. 8, 1939, and Hitler again made several flying front visits by G-4 like this one. Standing outside the security G-4 at left with hands clasped behind his back is Martin Bormann, while Hitler—map in left hand—shakes the hand of a local unit commander in the field with his right. (HHA, USNA, College Park, MD/USA.)

A *Führer* G-4 Front Column vehicle with machine gun in Poland, Sept. 10, 1939—passing Polish Army POWs heading in the opposite direction, into captivity. (HHA, USNA, College Park, MD/USA.)

A previously-unpublished photograph of the *Führer* gazing upward at a plinth-mounted bust of the late Polish Marshal Josef Pilsudski (1867-1935) in conquered Poland, September 1939, possibly at his Seat of Government, Castle Belvedere, in Warsaw, on 5 October. (HHA, USNA, College Park, MD/USA.)

The Nazi *Führer* (left) on a front visit at Maslow, Poland, on Sept. 10, 1939, with Hitler's Chief Military Adjutant—Col. Rudolf Schmundt—at center, carrying map case, and Front Column *Kommandant* Maj. Gen Erwin Rommel at far right. The *Führer's* new field gray uniform with British Army-style Sam Browne belt was reportedly designed for him as a surprise by his *SS* aides for his *Reichstag* war speech of Sept. 1, 1939. (HHA, USNA, College Park, MD/USA.)

The *Führer* (left) meets his Army Commander-in-Chief (right), Col. Gen. Walther von Brauchitsch (1881-1948), in Poland, with Gen. Walther von Reichenau (1884-1942) at center left, closer to Hitler. (HHA, USNA, College Park, MD/USA.)

Hitler (right) chats with his entourage in Poland, September 1939, from left to right: Col. Gen. Hans-Gunther von Kluge (1882-1944), Rommel, *SS* Maj. Gen. Julius Schaub, *RSD* chief Johann Rattenhuber, and Gen. Alfred Jodl. (HHA, USNA, College Park, MD/USA.)

A previously-unpublished photograph of former German Army Field Marshal "Clever Hans" von Kluge (left) talking with Army Gen. Ewald von Kleist (right) in Poland, September 1939. At far right is Jodl, at far left Hitler *SS* aide Hans-Georg Schulze-Kossens, and then Martin Bormann (wearing goggles on cap visor), with Hitler at center. The black scratches down the middle of the picture indicate that either Hitler or photographer Hoffmann didn't want it published. (HHA, USNA, College Park, MD/USA.)

A previously-unpublished photo of SS Maj. Gen. Julius Schaub wearing *Waffen SS* gray eating in Poland in September 1939 at the Front Column's mess truck. (HHA, USNA, College Park, MD/USA.)

A mystery photo identified? According to the late *FHQ* author/researcher Richard Raiber, MD of Hockessin, DE/USA, the *Führer* watched German Army artillery bombard the besieged Polish capital of Warsaw twice in September 1939 from a high elevation: on the 22nd from a church steeple at Gliniki, and again—on the 25th—from a tower at Stucewice. I have concluded that this scene shows the first occasion, with Hitler third from left and Keitel sixth from left, with goggles on his cap visor. On the other hand, stated David Irving in his 1977 work *Hitler's War*, "On the 25th, Hitler had visited the 10th and 8th Armies; the latter had 150 batteries of artillery drawn up for the final bombardment due to begin next day. From the roof of a sports stadium, Hitler and a handful of his followers watched with binoculars as the artillery pounded Warsaw…." (HHA, USNA, College Park, MD/USA.)

On Sept. 10, 1939, the *Führer* visits 10th Army headquarters at Bialaczow, from left to right: Keitel, unknown *SS* officer, Hitler, Rommel, Rattenhuber (wearing goggles on his cap), and von Reichenau (with view finder). (HHA, USNA, College Park, MD/USA.)

A trio of previously-unpublished views of the same event, a Polish Front Column visit by the *Führer* on Sept.10, 1939, showing at center from left to right: Rommel, Hitler, and von Reichenau, as seen from the rear of one of the G-4 escort cars. (HHA, USNA, College Park, MD/USA.)

#173

#174

This page and following: A series of six shots from the very same Hitler Front Column visit in Poland, Sept. 23, 1939. In **#173**, Hitler (center) stresses a point for a listening Rommel at far right. In **#174**, from left to right are seen Keitel, Hitler, Capt. Gerhard Engel in left profile and soft garrison cap, Rommel (with map under his left arm), and Hitler *SA* adjutant Wilhelm Brückner, wearing Army uniform. In **#175**, from left to right are Hitler, Schaub, Rommel, von Reichenau, and Engel. In **#176**, from left to right are Jodl, Rommel, Martin Bormann, Hitler, 18th Army Infantry Division commander Crantz (according to *FHQ* author Aaron L. Johnson), and Capt. Engel (1906-76), the *Führer's* Army adjutant during 1938-43. An artillery officer, Engel had originally been adjutant to the former Commander-in-Chief of the Army, Baron Col. Gen. Werner von Fritsch. He ended the war as a major general commanding the 12th *Volks* (*People's*) Grenadier Division in the final battles to save the Reich in 1945. Maj. Gen. Engel died on Dec. 9, 1976, at Dusseldorf. In 2005, his memoirs were published as *At the Heart of the Reich: The Secret Diary of Hitler's Army Adjutant*. In **#177**, from left to right are Martin Bormann, Rommel, Max Wünsche, Hitler, Jodl, and von Reichenau. In **#178**, from left to right are seen two unknown Army officers, Hitler, *Luftwaffe* Gen. Karl Bodenschatz, von Reichenau, unidentified Army officer, Rommel, and a third unknown Army officer. According to British revisionist author David Irving, Bormann and the later famous Desert Fox became bitter personal enemies on this wartime tour in Poland. The Front Column *Kommandant* crossed swords with Bormann when Hitler visited the captured Polish port city of Gdynia. As the column tried to drive down a narrow street, Rommel bawled out, "Only the *Führer's* car will drive down! The rest will wait here!" Bormann's third car attempted to follow, but Rommel stood in the way, and Bormann demanded entry. Rommel shouted, "I am headquarters commandant. This is not a kindergarten outing, and you will do as I say!" Thus, Rommel made a powerful enemy within Hitler's inner circle. (HHA, USNA, College Park, MD/USA.)

#175

#176

#177

#178

#179

#180

A famous series of newsreel stills of Hitler watching the 14th German Army crossing the San River at Jaroslaw on Sept. 15, 1939, all from the exact same vantage point. **#179** is a filmstrip shot by the *Führer's Luftwaffe* motion picture lensman, the late Walter Frentz (1907-2004.) In **#s183** and **184** Jodl is seen at the far right of the frames, while in **#182**, Martin Bormann is seen at the center of the cluster of officers on the embankment. Noted Prof. Heinrich Hoffmann in his 1955 memoir *Hitler was My Friend* "I traveled with Hitler and his staff to the Polish front in the Special Train…From there, he was able to follow the progress of the German armies, and each day—either by aircraft or with a small protective motorized column—we went up to some part of the front line. These drives were by no means without danger, for large bodies of disintegrated Polish cavalry had taken refuge in the woods on either side of the roads. Had they but known who was traveling with the diminutive column, and had they but realized the weakness of the protective pickets—one rifleman every 100 yards—it would've been the easiest thing in the world for them to have destroyed Hitler and the whole of his entourage. We had a number of lucky escapes and narrow shaves, but our luck held, and we came through unscathed: and for myself—at the risk of being thought somewhat irreverent—I must confess I got a bit bored with hearing again and again how mercifully Providence was protecting us!" (As Hitler himself boasted.) (HHA, USNA, College Park, MD/USA.)

#181

#182

#183

#184

The *Führer's* G-4 motorcade enters Oliva on his visit to Danzig on Sept. 19, 1939. (HHA, USNA, College Park, MD/USA.)

Hitler's G-4 begins its first stop of Sept. 19, 1939, with a pre-Danzig stop to visit the crew of the German Navy battleship *Schleswig-Holstein*, which started the German-Polish war by firing on the Poles' fortress at Westerplatte. The ship was named for the Danish province seized by the Kingdom of Prussia in 1864. The *Führer* got to and from the ship by a launch, and departed by car, the way he'd arrived. Here the Naval honor guard salutes as the vehicle pulls away. According to John H. Bloecher, Jr., of the Danzig Study Group, Baltimore, MD/USA, "The *Schleswig-Holstein* is moored at Neufahrwasser, and Hitler takes off from his review and heads for the city." (HHA, USNA, College Park, MD/USA.)

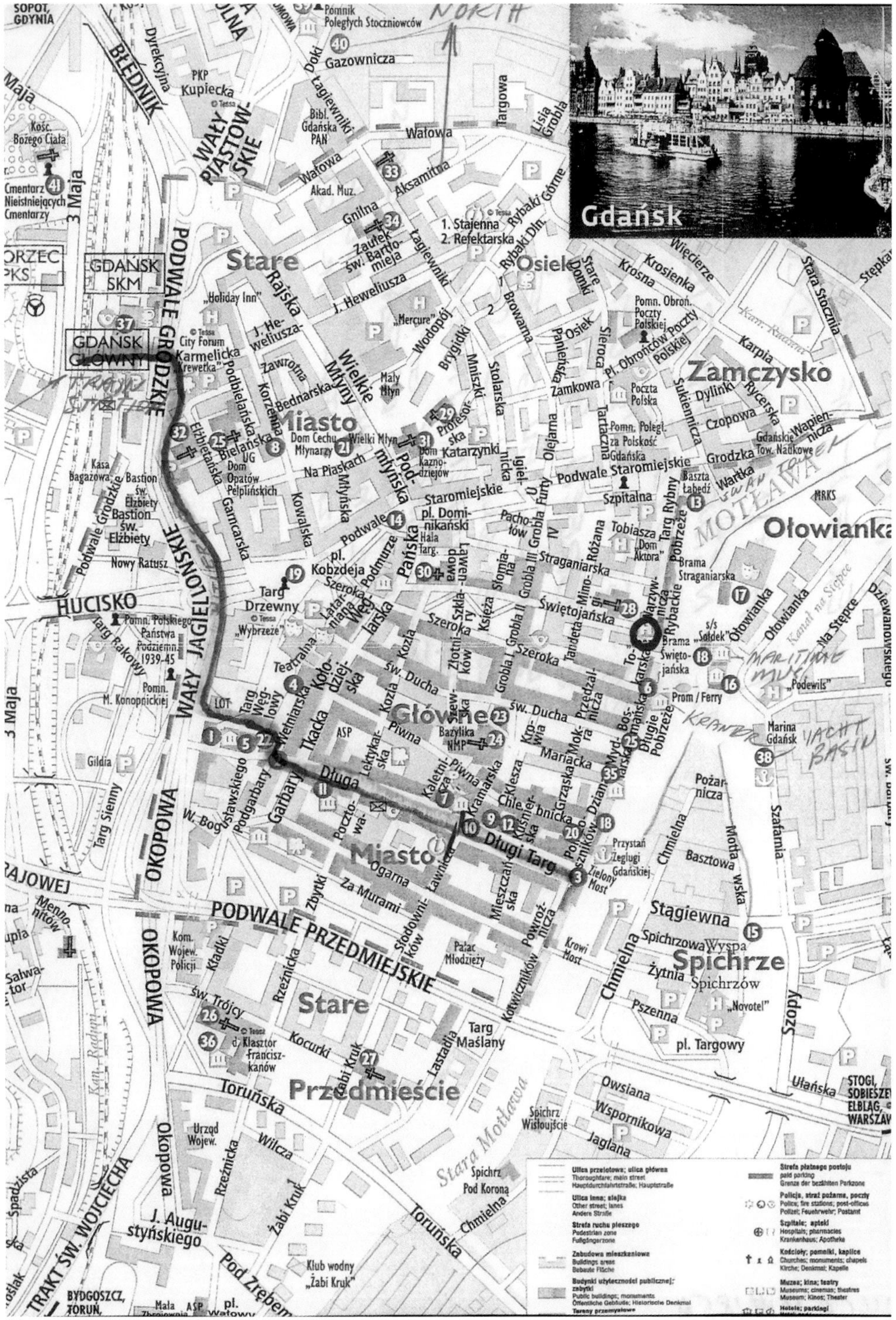

A good map of Hitler's parade route through German-liberated Danzig on Tuesday, Sept. 19, 1939. States John H. Bloecher, Jr., of the Danzig Study Group, Baltimore, MD/USA, "The parade route on the map begins at the west end of the Langgasse, and ends at the eastern end at the *Rathaus/City Hall*, a block west of the Green Gate. The triumphal parades always started at the High Gate, around the Prison and Torture Chamber, then through the Langgasse Gate into the Langgasse, terminating at the *Rathaus* or Green Gate. In Hitler's case, it was at the *Rathaus*, and he walked the final distance to the *Artushof* [*King Arthur's Court* or *House of King Arthur*]," named for the ancient Briton monarch of legend and lore! The numbers shown here on the map correspond, according to Mr. Bloecher, to the following sites: "1) *Rathaus*, 10) extent of Langmarkt (Dlugi Targ), 9) *Artushof*, 12) Nazi Party headquarters in Danzig, 6) Krantor, 28) St. John's Church 3) Green Gate with bridge, 15) Milk Can Gate, 20) English House, 24) *Marienkirche* (*Marien Church*), 35) St. Mary's Gate, at east end of Frauengasse; H) Hansa Hotel. "Gdansk" (upper right) is the Polish name for the German Danzig, and is 1 ½ miles by boat over water to Westerplatte." (Danzig Study Group, Baltimore, MD/USA.)

Opposite: A modern day view of the Tuesday, Sept. 19, 1939, Hitlerian parade route as it appears today. (Danzig Study Group, Baltimore, MD/USA.)

Jaka
jest historia
tego miejsca?

On Tuesday, Sept. 19, 1939, the *Führer* entered now-German Danzig in triumph during the victorious military campaign against Poland in a G-4 heading up a whole column of other G-4s, with a pair of RSD cars immediately following his own. According to John H. Bloecher, Jr., of the DSG, "Motorcade heads south on what *may* be the Reichsbank on the Stadtgraben, although the photo doesn't show the roof lines clearly enough to identify. Our copy is almost a silhouette with no details." (HHA, USNA, College Park, MD/USA.)

Hitler's G-4 has turned from the main road (the Dluga) from the railroad station into Langgasse, about one mile and a quarter to the *Artushof*, where the *Führer* gave a victory speech. According to John H. Bloecher, Jr., of the DSG, "Langgasse is the correct name of the *Royal Road* that leads from the Langgasse Tor (Gate) to the Green Gate at the river. Usually spelled as Langgasse on the maps. There are no strasse designations in Danzig. The first block in the east widens to the Langemarkt (Lange Market). Here, Hitler's motorcade turns east through the Langgasse Gate and east on the Langgasse. Statue of Kaiser Wilhelm (I) is at right with the Hotel Danziger Hof at extreme left. The loss of that hotel is lamented by Germans and Poles alike." (HHA, USNA, College Park, MD/USA.)

According to John H. Bloecher, Jr., of the DSG, "A welcoming scene along the Langgasse." A view of Hitler's entry into Danzig on Sept. 19, 1939, as "Great crowds filled the pavements and the windows and balconies," according to one source. Note the pylons along the building fronts at left with gilded Nazi eagles atop and the crowned crest of the city on their facades. The backup RSD G-4s can also be seen. (HHA, USNA, College Park, MD/USA.)

"One People, One Nation, One Leader!" asserts the overhead banner in the distance as Hitler rides over flower-strewn streets in Danzig—an honor he would not be accorded in the Reich until his victory entry into Berlin on July 6, 1940. On Sept. 12, 1939, the *Führer's* Adjutants' Office released a bulletin stating, "The *Führer* will not accept flowers on his trips for the duration of the war. Any flowers intended for him should be given to the soldiers of the German *Wehrmacht*.'" Note the positioning of the RSD cars behind him in this picture. According to *After the Battle's The Third Reich: Then and Now*, "This is the main street called Dluga..." Adds John H. Bloecher, Jr., of the DSG, "The procession is now entering the old city, with the Langgasse Gate and the Stockturm in the background, separated by 60 yards. This route was once known as the *Royal Road*." (HHA, USNA, College Park, MD/USA.)

On Tuesday, Sept. 19, 1939, Hitler received a tumultuous welcome from the delirious German residents of liberated Danzig (today Gdansk, Poland.) Here, followed by two G-4 Escort cars at a distance, Hitler's car passes the railway station between Karrenwall and Horst-Hoffmannwall. Today, the streets are called Okopowa and 3 Maja in Polish. As I wrote in my1999 work *Mercedes-Benz Parade and Staff Cars of the Third Reich*, "*After the Battle* magazine says that this shot shows the motorcade reaching the square outside the *Artushof*. According to John H. Bloecher, Jr., of the DSG, 'This scene shows the procession heading east on the Langgasse. The destination is the *Artushof*, just beyond the *Rathaus* [*City Hall*] is the tall tower with the clock at left, while the main German Post Office is the multi-story brick building at center right. The banner says, in German, 'Our Faith in Your Ideology to Victory!' Motorcade is nearing the City Hall; its bell tower and clock tower is in left background… Most of the buildings are small shops and restaurants on this street." (HHA, USNA, College Park, MD/USA.)

"Danzig greets its Leader!" the overhead banner proclaims as Hitler's G-4 car enters the city in triumph on Sept. 19, 1939. Adds John H. Bloecher, Jr., of the DSG, "View from in front of the City Hall, looking west. The procession is nearing its destination," which is the *Artushof*. (HHA, USNA, College Park, MD/USA.)

According to *After the Battle's The Third Reich: Then and Now*, "The convoy halts outside the *Artushof*, where Hitler was due to speak." In this shot, according to John H. Bloecher, Jr., of the DSG, "The Green Gate is at the left, while the *Artushof* is also on the left side, behind the fountain. The plaza and street are known as the *Langtmarkt*. The view from this vantage point is looking east." The scene is from the rear of two cars full of RSD men—as others are on foot behind them—with Hitler standing in his car in the distance at center. (HHA, USNA. College Park, MD/USA.)

States John H. Bloecher, Jr., of the DSG, "Final destination—*Gauleiter* [*Regional Leader*] Albert Forster (center) greets his *Führer* in front of the *Rechtstadtische Rathaus* [*Main Town City Hall*]. They are just 50 yards from the entrance to the *Artushof* from which Hitler makes his speech." Adds the late American author John Toland, "Hitler's triumphal entry into Danzig on Sept. 19th. 'Almighty God,' he told a partisan crowd, 'has now blessed our weapons.'" (HHA, USNA, College Park, MD/USA.)

A very rare view of the *Führer* and his entourage walking from the line of G-4s (right) from the *Rathaus* to the Danzig *Artushof* on Dluga Street, past the Neptune Fountain on Sept. 19, 1939, as originally seen in the 2005 work by Jerzy Kuklinski, *Gdansk: Past and Present*, which states, "In *Artus Court*, he made a speech in which he tried to justify using violence against Poland. At the end, he said, 'Gdansk was German, Gdansk remained German, and from this moment on, it will be German as long as the German nation and the German Reich exist,' or—as it turned out—until 1945." I also rather think that he used the term 'Danzig' rather than Gdansk! Hitler is at center, and at right are Nazi leaders Albert Forster and Artur Greiser. (DSG)

States John H. Bloecher, Jr., of the DSG of this modern view, "The front entrance to the *Artushof*, with (King) Neptune's Fountain in the right foreground with the entrance to the underground restaurant with the figure of Mercury on top (far left)." (DSG photo)

#1

This page and following: Asserts John H. Bloecher, Jr., in the *Danzig Study Report #134 October-November-December 2006*, "One auditorium, 3 almost simultaneous photos. Here's what started the ball rolling…a previously-unpublished photo **(1)** by Heinrich Hoffmann from our author/friend Blaine Taylor. Compare the camera location with Giles' photo **(2)** with name on back in violet ink: FRANZ BRAUN PHOT./DANZIGER. Photo **(3)** is from the 1975 *Danziger Hauskalender*. The cameraman is close to the back of the room in this shot," the entire trio being taken in the *Artushof*, Sept. 19, 1939. Stated *After the Battle's The Third Reich: Then and Now*, "American CBS correspondent William L. Shirer was one of those present: 'I had a seat on the aisle, and as he strode past me to the rostrum, I thought that he (Hitler) looked more imperious than I had ever seen him. Also, he was about as angry during his speech as I've ever seen him. When he spoke of Britain, his face flamed up in hysterical rage. Afterwards, a Nazi acquaintance confided to me that the 'old man' was in a terrible rage because he had counted on making today's speech in Warsaw, that he had waited three or four days outside the Polish capital, burning to enter it like a conquering Caesar and make his speech of victory, and that when the Poles inside refused to surrender and each day continued their stubborn resistance, his patience had cracked and he rushed to Danzig to make his speech." Hitler stated, "I have no war aims against England and France…have the honor to stand here as representative of this regime (the German government). It is for me the greatest honor to be regarded in that way….If it lasts three years, the word capitulation will not arise on our side, nor in the fourth, fifth, sixth, and seventh years…About one thing there can be no doubt—we are taking up the challenge!" He was as good as his word on this score. (HHA, USNA, College Park, MD; and Danzig Study Group, Baltimore, MD/USA.)

#2

#3

The *Führer* and his immediate staff emerge from one of the buildings on the grounds of *FHQ* Zoppot's Kasino Hotel at Danzig on Sept. 23, 1939. From left to right: Rommel with maps, Dr. Hans Heinrich Lammers, Hitler, Engel, Schmundt, Bodenschatz, and an unknown officer. Note the G-4 at the lower right of the frame! Recalled Prof. Hoffmann in 1955, "When we returned late each night to headquarters, we were so filthy and covered with the yellow dust of the Polish roads, that we were unrecognizable…During the campaign, I did not obtain nearly as many really good photographs as one would expect from an experienced press photographer; nevertheless, those which I succeeded in getting were incorporated into a volume, *With Hitler in Poland*, and make a valuable contribution to the pictorial history of the war." According to David Irving, it was at *FHQ* Zoppot that Hitler formulated his 1940 plans to introduce euthanasia mercy killing in Germany as a prelude to the later, fuller implementation of the Final Solution of the Jewish Question. Zoppot is now Sopot, Poland. (HHA, USNA, College Park, MD/USA.)

A good frontal view of Hitler's G-4 in Poland showing the headlamps covered for wartime use. Although the license plates were all covered for security purposes throughout the *Führer* Column according to Dr. Peter Hoffmann, note that the *Führerstandarte* is clearly evident! The passengers are Hitler and *SS* driver Erich Kempka in front, adjutant Col. Rudolf Schmundt, and Army Gen. Walter von Reichenau (later a field marshal) in the middle, with RSD man Hans Junge, Army Adjutant Capt. Erhard Engel, and *Luftwaffe* aide Col. Nikolaus von Below in the back. Despite the rigid security guidelines that were supposed to be in effect, on several occasions during the Polish campaign, Hitler's car was mobbed by friendly German soldiers—or truckloads of sullen Polish POWs going in the opposite direction. (HHA, USNA, College Park, MD/USA.)

Hitler (left) examines a captured Polish guidon banner, in company with, from left to right, *SS* Maj. Gen. Julius Schaub, Dr. Otto Dietrich, and *RFSS* Heinrich Himmler (in left profile). (HHA, USNA, College Park, MD/USA.)

A previously-unpublished photograph of a rainy lunch in the field under a tent and rain capes at the G-4 *Führer* Column mess truck. From left to right are seen unknown officer (back to camera), *RFSS* Himmler (facing the lens), Hitler, and Martin Bormann (hand on left hip.) (HHA, USNA, College Park, MD/USA.)

A previously-unpublished photograph of a typical Hitler Front visit to the field in Poland, September 1939, from left to right: *RFSS* Heinrich Himmler (holding his glasses), unknown Army officer, Hitler, and another unidentified Army officer. (HHA, USNA, College Park, MD/USA.)

The *Führer* comes calling on Sept. 25, 1939, on *SS* Gen. Josef "Sepp" Dietrich's *LSSAH* Regiment: this had been its babtism of fire against the Polish Army. From left to right are Sepp, Hitler's *SS* ordnance officer Max Wünsche, the *Führer*, Col. Schmundt, and an escort officer holding the G-4's door at far right. Note also the nighttime driving lamp cover just below the door. So far as is known, no Front Column was ever strafed by either enemy or friendly aircraft throughout the entire war—a fate that befell Erwin Rommel, Sepp himself, Grand Adm. Karl Donitz, and Army Field Marshal Fedor von Bock, among others. With Hitler in Poland, bombs were dropped only two-three kilometers away, presumably by the Polish Air Force. The Leader Column then withdrew. (HHA., USNA, College Park, MD/USA.)

Hitler (left) reviews the First Company of the *SSLAH* in Poland, Sept. 25, 1939. (HHA, USNA, College Park, MD/USA.)

A previously-unpublished photo of Sepp Dietrich (left) and *RFSS* Heinrich Himmler (right) during the *Führer's* visit of Sept. 25, 1939, in Poland. There was, reportedly, little love lost between the two top *SS* commanders, especially as Sepp reported directly to Hitler himself, not to the *RFSS*. The reason was that Hitler—rightly, as it turned out—trusted Sepp more with his personal security than he did Himmler, a traitor in 1945, and maybe also in 1934 and 1939. (HHA, USNA, College Park, MD/USA.)

A pair of very similar—but slightly different—shots, the first of which is previously-unpublished. The scene is the airfield at Kielce, Poland, Sept. 10, 1939, with, from left to right, Rommel, von Reichenau, Brückner, and Hitler—but no bodyguards in sight. (HHA, USNA, College Park, MD/USA.)

Hitler's rather somber entry onto the deserted streets of the conquered Polish capital, Warsaw, on Oct. 5, 1939, for his sole victory parade on enemy territory of the entire war. All the headlamp covers of his own G-4—as well as the security car following at right, but *not* that at left—are covered. Hitler stands up in front—just as in Austria and Czechslovakia before—with *SS* driver Erich Kempka again at the steering wheel. *SS* valet Heinz Linge sits atop the folded down hood at rear, while the escort guards have their machine guns at the ready, in case of trouble. There *was* no Nazi Dallas, however, as Hitler's cars were never fired upon during wartime, so far as is known to date. (HHA, USNA, College Park, MD/USA.)

A view of the two-hour German victory parade in Warsaw of Oct. 5, 1939, of the reviewing stand, as seen from across Ujazdowska Street from the vantage point of the Dutch Embassy. Hitler (right) stands giving a rigid-armed Nazi salute from under the tree at the left. The rather puny-looking Pzkpfw I tanks "Did not prove very durable in combat," according to author Steven J. Zaloga's 2002 work *Poland 1939: The Birth of Blitzkrieg.* "Its armor could be easily penetrated by Polish anti-tank rifles or 37mm anti-tank guns." (*Signal,* George Peterson, National Capital Historic Sales, Springfield, VA/USA.)

A famous close-up view of the reviewing stand, with the trees as a backdrop. Hitler stands in leather overcoat at left, hands clasped in front, with German Army Gen. Johannes Blaskowitz seen biting his lip at far right. He had reason to, as his formal protests against the *SS* atrocities in Poland he'd witnessed cost him—in his view, at least—ever being awarded the coveted field marshal's baton from an angry *Führer.* In this scene, German Army bicyclists (!) are walking by at the left. Gen. Wilhelm Keitel stands third from right, seen in left profile. (Walther Frentz.)

A view from behind Hitler of the parade and of the Dutch Embassy across Warsaw's Ujazdowska Street. If you look *very* closely at the back of Hitler's cap, you can see where the wraparound golden cord *almost* meets at the top, but not quite! (Walter Frentz)

Hitler's own view of the German Army troops goose-stepping past him on Ujasdowska Street in Warsaw during the German victory parade of Oct. 5, 1939, with troops also drawn up in single file outside the Dutch Embassy across the road. (Walter Frentz)

Gen. Wilhelm Keitel (right front seat) grins at the lensman from a G-4 full of his own staff members. (HHA, USNA, College Park, MD/USA.)

5

Furor Teutonicus! Western and Balkan Fronts 1940-41

On the evening of May 9, 1940, Reich Photo Reporter Prof. Heinrich Hoffmann and Reich Chancellor Adolf Hitler slipped out the back door of the *New German Reich Chancellery* in Berlin bound for a secret destination, as the former recalled in his 1955 memoirs, *Hitler Was My Friend*:

"'Where to Hitler, Norway?' Hoffmann asked in a whisper. 'Yes! Who told you?' 'No one told me. I'm just guessing.' 'Right, but not a word to anyone else, Hoffmann!'

"The (car) convoy set off in the direction of Staaken Airport, but to everybody's surprise, did not stop there, and drove straight on. Only the last car stopped, to bar the road to all on-coming traffic. On we went, and it seemed as though we were intending to make the whole journey by car.

"Suddenly, however, we pulled up at a closed level crossing; and beside it stood the *Führer's* Special Train...Speculation was rife. We were traveling in the direction of Hamburg, and the consensus of opinion was in favor of Norway (which had been invaded, along with tiny Denmark, on the previous Apr. 9th by the German Army and Navy)....

"The next dawn, Hitler made a surprise and rare appearance at breakfast, pulled out his watch, and announced, 'Gentlemen, it's exactly 5:45 AM—the first shots are being fired—now!'... It was May 10, 1940. The offensive in the West had started! Another of Hitler's surprise packets!...

"In the bright sunshine, we reached Euskirchen, near Cologne, where we changed into the waiting (G-4) cars. An hour later, we arrived at the *Felsennest* [*Rocky Nest*], the first of the *Führer Headquarters* (*FHQ*), near Munster on the Eifel [in Germany]...."

According to David Irving in his 1977 study *Hitler's War*:

"An hour before dawn, at 4:25 AM, the train glided into a small station...It was Euskirchen, 30 miles from the Allied lines. A column of the three-axle field limousines that had served Hitler so well in Poland was awaiting him in the semidarkness. For half an hour, he and his entourage drove through the little Eifel villages, in which the signposts had been replaced by stark yellow plates with various military symbols on them.

"Hitler broke the silence only once. Turning to Maj. von Below, the *Luftwaffe* adjutant sitting with Schaub on the jump seats of his car, he asked, 'Has the *Luftwaffe* taken into account that here in the West the sun rises several minutes later than in Berlin?' Below set his mind at rest.

"After a while, the country lanes began to climb a hill through scattered woods. When his limousine stopped, Hitler clambered stiffly out....His field headquarters...From the two main roads in the valleys on each side of this hill, they could hear the heavy rumble of convoys of trucks heading westward."

Hitler remained there from 10 May to 6 June, then relocated to *FHQ Wolfsschlucht* (*Wolf's Gorge*) at Brûly-de-Pesche, Belgium, from 6-25 June, then changed locations again to *Tannenberg* (*Pine Mountain*), in Germany's famous Black Forest, during June 28-July 5, 1940, the third and final Western Campaign *FHQ*.

During this period, Hitler made a number of wartime front visits by G-4 car convoy as in Poland previously. Writing in *Hitler's Military Headquarters, FHQ* author Aaron L. Johnson noted the following dates and locations of Hitler's trips outside Nazi Germany:

"May 24th, Charleville; June 2nd, Langemarck, Vimy Heights (Ridge), Loretto; June 21st, Compiegne; June 23rd, Paris; June 26th-27th, Northern France" (visiting his old World War I sites); June 29th; Strasbourg;-Schlettstsadt; June 30th, Muhlhausen and Upper Alsace," leaving out his most famous, first Western Campaign drive: to Bastogne, Belgium, on 17 May to visit the headquarters of German Army Group A under Col. Gen. Gerd von Rundstedt.

This famed road convoy *Führer* Gray Column visit is recounted in some detail in Gen. Walter Warlimont's 1964 work *Inside Hitler's Headquarters*:

"Although he had played a considerable part in the bold conception of the armored operation, he now became obsessed with the protection of the flank...and hurried off himself that same afternoon [17 May] by road to Bastogne to emphasize his preoccupations to the Commander-in-Chief...von Rundstedt.

"There he said that under no circumstances must there be any form of setback at this moment, since that would be a dangerous morale-raiser for the enemy. At the moment, the decision depended not so much on a rapid thrust to the Channel, as in the ability to secure as quickly as possible an absolutely sound *defense* on the Aisne (River), and later on the Somme (River), even if it involved temporary delay of the advance to the West.

"By the evening of May 17th, therefore (Army Chief of Staff Gen. Franz) Halder had become worried; he writes: 'A most unfortunate day. The *Führer* is terribly nervous. He is frightened by his own success, is unwilling to take any risks, and is trying to hold us back.'"

The moment passed, however, the Channel was reached, the British Expeditionary Force escaped by sea, Paris fell, and the French Army surrendered.

Adds Dr. Peter Hoffmann in his 1979 study *Hitler's Personal Security: Protecting the Führer, 1921-45,* the *Führer* Special Train:

"Arrived at Euskirchen station ay 4:25 AM on May 10th...The *Führer* had himself driven to his *Felsennest* HQ in Rodert at once.

"Three convoys were organized to accompany the *Führer* on his tours of the front, so that they could be ordered quickly to distant places. A typical convoy—or *Frontgruppe* [*Front Group*]—of the *Führer-Begleit-Battalion* in May 1940 consisted of elements of an infantry company, of a signal corps unit, of a motorcycle platoon, of an armored reconnaissance platoon including a radio car, a machine gun car, two cars carrying 2 cm guns, two anti-aircraft platoons, two field kitchens, two fuel tankers, (and) parts of supply sections.

"This little army surrounded—preceding and following—15 cars of what was now known as a Gray Column, carrying Hitler and his party. The other two groups contained, in addition, two sets with essentially the same details as the first, 19 Gray Column cars, plus a Fieseler *Storch* [*Stork*] (light aircraft), and 14 Gray Column cars, respectively.

"They and the rest of the *Führer-Begleit-Battalion (FBB)* were commanded by the HQ Commandant. Maj. Gen. Rommel had been given a new post, and had been replaced by Lt. Col. Thomas as *FHQ* Commandant...

"It was a while before Hitler was able to inspect his conquests on the Western Front. During the first days of the campaign, the roads in Belgium were still full of mines, and not safe for travel.

"On May 15th, 16th, and 18th, reconnaissance detachments of the *FBB* sent out to collect information on the state of the roads reported the rest west of Limburg was under artillery fire. One of Hitler's armored Mercedes cars was being kept ready at Bastogne airfield, along with two three-axle cars (G-4s) for his *FBK*, and two for the immediate military entourage, plus one car in reserve

"The leader in this small group was told to get in touch with Lt. Col. (Henning) von Tresckow to find a good place for parking the Gray Column cars—the same officer who was to become the driving force behind the assassination attempts in 1943.

"Hitler took his first trip to the Western Front on May 17th, when he flew to Bastogne to meet the staff of Army Group A...A convoy of cars took him with his suite to Odendorf airfield; they flew to Bastogne airfield, motored about in a convoy sent for this purpose, and returned to *Felsennest* HQ the same evening.

"A longer trip to the front was taken on June 1st and 2nd. Several *FBB* detachments were sent ahead to Brussels airport and to Tournai. At the airport, three motor convoys were kept available from which the travel group was to be composed. They included a car for the *Führer*, two for his escort details, one for adjutants, and one for Keitel, also a group of motorcycle riflemen, an armored personnel carrier with an anti-aircraft gun, a radio squad, a press-radio car and armored reconnaissance radio car, field kitchen, and supply and luggage car.

"When the HQ Commandant went ahead to reconnoiter and find suitable quarters, fighting was still in progress in the southwest sections of Lille (30 May)...At 9 AM, Hitler and his party left *Felsennest* HQ for Odendorf airfield, from where they flew off to Brussels at 10 AM on June 1st.

"At Brussels airfield the travelers were met by Gen. (Fedor) von Bock, Commander-in-Chief of Army Group B, who reported the situation to the *Führer.* Hitler went on through Brussels to Ghent, Courtrai, and Bisseghem in the customary order, with two carloads of his *SS* and RSD escort following him directly, and with Bormann, (Dr. Otto) Dietrich, Brandt, Hewell, Morell, also adjutants, and finally Keitel and his aides following.

"At a distance of 1 kilometer, there followed an anti-aircraft battery, radio cars, field kitchen, and supply cars...Then the party visited the battlefields and German military cemeteries at Ypres and Langemarck, and finally went to *(FHQ)* Chateau de Brigode for the night.

"Next day, Hitler visited Avelin, Vimy, Arras, Douai, Bouchain, and Cambrai, from where he took his plane to Charleville. Here, Gen. von Rundstedt reported to him. By 6:30 PM, he was back in *Felsennest.*

"...On June 21st, Hitler motored to the (French) forest of Compiegne. Here the German armistice conditions were to be presented to the French High Command...Then Hitler and his suite left and returned to *Wolfsschlucht* the same evening....Hitler paid a secret visit to Paris early in the morning of June 23rd...

"At 3:30 AM the party took off from Gros Caillou airfield and flew to Le Bourget. In five cars—with the usual *SS* and RSD escort—the group drove into Paris in the haze of the early morning. There was no cordoning off...The tour took the group to the Champs-Elysees, past the Madeleine to the Trocadero, and to the Eiffel Tower, where they got out and walked a bit, then to the Tomb of the Unknown Soldier, and to the Domedes Invalides, where Hitler stood and mused at Napoleon's Tomb.

"On to the Pantheon, Place des Vosges, the Louvre, the Palais de Justice, Sainte Chapelle, down the Rue de Rivoli, and finally to the monstrosity of Sacre Coeur on Montmartre. By about 9 AM, the entire visit was over, after no more than three hours. A number of people had recognized Hitler, but had ignored him or run away. A market woman had exclaimed, 'It's him—oh, it's him!' before she fled.

"By 11 AM, Hitler was back in *Wolfsschlucht*, and soon began preparations for the invasion of Britain, and at the same time for an attack on Russia....Some more tours of battlefields in France followed, some from an HQ in the Black Forest, *Tannenberg*, late in June and early in July 1940.

"Security was reduced to a minimum. It was fairly safe to count on secrecy and surprise, but there were anxious moments for the bodyguard when the *Führer's* small convoy of four or five open Mercedes cars passed a thinly-guarded column of thousands of French prisoners-of-war marching in the opposite direction...."

As I wrote in the January 2002 Premier Issue of *WWII History* Magazine in my article "Furor Teutonicus and Gallic Debacle":

"According to (French writer Jean-Paul) Pallud, the victorious Germans lost 27,704 men killed, 111,034 wounded, and 18,384 missing and considered probably killed…The BEF—with 250,000 men at the outset on May 10th—lost a comparatively light figure of 3,457 killed and 13,602 wounded. Predictably…the French again were the campaign's big losers, with 92,000 killed, 250,000 wounded, and 1,450,000 prisoners-of-war…."

According to the late Dr. Richard Raiber's previously-unpublished manuscript *FührerBegleit-Battalion Frontgruppen*:

"The campaign in the West began on May 10, 1940, and it was again foreseen that the *FBB* would be expected to assign front groups for Hitler's tours of the front.

"Several convoys of *SS*-driven G-4s—now known as *Grau Kolonne* [*Gray Columns*]— were organized and prepared for this purpose…

"However, the front advanced rapidly, so that the distances between the *FHQu* and the objectives of Hitler's tours soon—as in Poland—required new tactics for the front groups. On May 22nd, several front groups were sent out into Belgium in order to be available where and when needed.

"Capt. Otto von Blomberg, Chief 1st Company, led his front group to Charleville, Belgium; Front Group (Capt. Alfred) Naehring (Chief, 3rd Company) went to Aachen, Germany; and Front Group (Capt. Walther) Barg, Chief of the Flak Battery, was sent to Brûly-de-Pesche, south of Philippeville in southern Belgium, where the site for a new *FHQ* had been chosen.

"On May 29th, Hitler's intention to tour the front in Flanders and Artois was announced. Front Group (FG) Naehring was ordered to shift from Aachen to Brussels, receive his aircraft, and provide military escort for the Gray Column. FG Blomberg was sent to the area between St. Amand and Tournai, Belgium: its mission would be to set up security at a site where the *Führer* column would stop overnight, June 1st-2nd.

"There was still fighting in Lille when the *Kommandant*—reconnoitering on May 30th for an appropriate site—selected the Chateua de Brigode at Annapes, six kilometers east of Lille. The battle had ended by the time FG Blomberg moved in next day…

"At 10 AM, June 1, 1940, Hitler flew from Odendorf to Brussels…Von Bock was there to greet him. In bright, sunny weather and under the protection of FG Naehring, Hitler and his associates boarded G-4s of the Gray Column, and the convoy proceeded westward through Ghent to Courtrai, Bisseghem, Ypres, and Langemarck (where Hitler stood in silence at the German First World War cemetery); Poperhinghe, Kemmel, Wervicq, and Menin (where the *Kommandant* joined the front group), Lille, and arrived at (*FHQ*) Chateau de Brigode at 7:20 PM.

"At 8:30 AM, June 2nd, the G-4s took Hitler and the others into Lille, where they viewed the city from the top of its citadel. The *Führer* column was then off to Pont a Marcq, Avelin, Seclin, Carvin, Lens, Vimy Ridge, Neuville, Souchez, Loretto Heights, Arras, Douai, Bouchain, and in early afternoon arrived at an airfield south of Cambrai.

"On both days Hitler had made several stops to visit high-level field commanders, and also to reminisce at points where he had served in the First World War. His June 1st-2nd itinerary clearly shows that he had participated in some of the bloodiest battles in that war.

"The travelers lunched at a field kitchen at the airfield…He visited troops over the holidays again in 1940, this time in Occupied France, under the protection of FGs assigned from the *FBK*. On Dec. 16, 1940, the battalion received notification of the *Führer's* projected front tour [by train] as well as to furnish motorized escorts for the G-4s whenever Hitler left the train.

"Two Gray Columns—as usual driven by *SS* officers and non-commissioned officers belonging to the *SS-Begleitkommando*—were alerted. [They] departed in motor convoys from their German bases… On Dec. 23, 1940…Hitler, his entourage, and an *FBK* (escort) then boarded Gray Column G-4s, and—with FG escort—drove westward, over roads coated with slick, icy frost, through Ardres and Guines to Rinxent, near Marquise…

"The FG drove westward 15 kilometers to Cap Gris Nez. He viewed *Grosser Kurfurst/Great Elector*—one of the massive, ferroconcrete emplacements, recently installed—whose big guns were lobbing shells into southeast England. At Cap Gris Nez, it is only 33 cross-Channel kilometers between the European Continent and the white cliffs of Dover.

"In early afternoon, the Front Column headed south along the coast, so that Hitler could examine other long-distance batteries…At 3 PM , the Front Column reached Boulogne, and Hitler made a brief tour of the harbor…At 4 PM, the G-4s transported Hitler and the others to the station at Wimereux, five kilometers north of Boulogne…."

On Christmas Eve, December 24, 1940:

"At 11:30 AM, Hitler's Front Column proceeded to Desvres, 20 kilometers east of Boulogne, so that he could celebrate Christmas with Fighter Squadron 3…At 2:15 PM, the Front Column turned back toward the Channel coast, and at St. Etienne, a suburb of Boulogne, Hitler re-boarded *Amerika*…At 4:05 PM, he was taken by *Führer* Column—which had driven south from St. Etienne—to Chateau Port-le-Grand, between Noyelles-sur-Mer and Abbeville; there, at 4:20 PM, Hitler was the guest of Maj. Adolf Galland, leader of Fighter Squadron 26, who later became General of Fighters, and one of the *Luftwaffe's* foremost fighter pilots."

The current author interviewed Gen. "Dolfo" Galland several times in the late 1980s. On Christmas Day 1940 at 1:45 PM:

"The Front Column—stopping… so that Hitler could visit a *Luftwaffe* unit—drove to Greil, 42 kilometers southeast of Beauvais."

The next day, the 26th, Hitler arrived at Metz at 10 AM:

"In Gray Column G-4s, escorted by FG motorcyclists, he was taken for a short tour of the city and then to celebrate a (belated) Christmas with the *SS Leibstandarte* [*Bodyguard Adolf Hitler Division*], bivouacked in Metz since the conclusion of the campaign in France.

"At 1:15 PM, Hitler re-boarded *Amerika* at Metz station and departed eastward to arrive in Saarburg at 4 PM. G-4s of the Gray Column he had used on the Atlantic coast were waiting and—escorted by Lt. Spaeter's motorcycle platoon—visited troops of Infantry Regiments 125 and 126 in Saarburg, Lützelburg, and, finally, at Arzweilerm, between Saarburg and Zabern.

"At 6:55 PM, he climbed aboard *Amerika* at Arzweiler, and arrived in Berlin at noon, Dec. 27th."

Thus ended for Hitler, the Third Reich, and their G-4s the epochal year of Nazi victory of 1940!

The Balkan Campaigns, Spring 1941

Hitler's unplanned and entirely unexpected Balkan campaigns of Spring 1941 came about by chance. First, Mussolini invaded Greece on October 28, 1940, and was soon finding his Fascist Militia and Savoyard Regular Italian Army being not only ejected by the hardy Greeks, but also chased back into their starting points in Occupied Albania!

In addition, Hitler's much-ballyhooed signing of the Axis Pact with formerly neutral Yugoslavia on March 25, 1941, at Vienna was nullified when Belgrade, its capital, rose up in revolt on the night of the 26th-27th, overthrew their pro-Nazi signatory—Regent Prince Paul—and installed the boy King Peter in his place. Enraged, the Nazi *Führer* instantly decided to punish the hated Serbs by bombing their capital and invading their country.

This, in turn, was coupled with a German ground invasion of Greece, in order to stabilize the *Duce's* international prestige abroad and his domestic regime stability at home.

Thus, were Hitler's Spring 1941 twin Balkan campaigns launched on the spur of the moment, in turn setting back his timetable for the invasion of the Union of Soviet Socialist Republics by a crucial 10 weeks that would cost the German *Wehrmacht* dearly that fall and winter in front of Moscow, Leningrad, and elsewhere in the then embattled USSR.

According to Dr. Hoffmann, Hitler took his G-4s with him during his train travels to visit Mussolini, Spain's *Generalissimo* Francisco Franco, and Vichy French Chief of State Marshal Henri Petain in the early fall of 1940 as the *Duce's* Greek imbroglio unfolded:

"On Apr. 25, 1941, the Special (Train) departed with Hitler for Marburg in southern Styria (Austria). At Spielfeld-Strass, he transferred to his motor convoy and then returned to Mönichkirchen (Austria)," from which he directed the Balkan campaigns from *Führersonderzug Amerika* in their entirety, the last such time he ever did so.

"On Apr. 26th, the Special went to Marburg and Graz (Austria), and the *Führer* took a drive through Graz in his open (G-4) Mercedes to the great merriment of crowds standing in the rain...In Marburg, the *FBK* detail were forced to run alongside the *Führer's* car to keep the crowds at least at arm's length from it."

The late Dr. Raiber added:

"In April 1941...Front Groups from the *FBB* provided perimeter military security and Flak protection. On Apr. 26th, *Amerika* left Mönichkirchen and transported Hitler...to Marburg, Graz, and Klagenfurt. That same day—with the British presence in Greece slipping away, and Athens about to fall, the FGs packed up and departed for Berlin.

"At 6:30 PM, Apr. 28, 1941, *Amerika* arrived with Hitler in Berlin...."

Thus concluded the *Führer's* militarily successful Balkan campaigns, but which also created a new Southern Front there that bedeviled the Axis Pact occupiers for the rest of the war.

One of Hitler's G-4s (center) parked in front of a chalet-like garage *FHQ Adlerhorst* at Ziegenberg, Germany, late in 1939. Built for the *Führer* by his chief architect—Dr. Albert Speer—Hitler refused to use it as too grandiose, until he needed it for the 1944-45 Battle of the Bulge. (HHA)

A famous group photo of all Hitler's Nazi "band of brothers" in the military-political inner circle at *FHQ Felsennest* (*Rocky Nest*) 1940. From left to right, first row: Chief Adjutant Wilhelm Brückner, Dr. Otto Dietrich, Gen. Wilhelm Keitel, Hitler, Gen. Alfred Jodl, Martin Bormann, *Luftwaffe* adjutant Maj. Nickolaus von Below, and Reich Photo Reporter Prof. Heinrich Hoffmann. Second row: Army adjutant Capt. Gerhard Engel, *SS* physician Dr. Karl Brandt, naval aide Rear Adm. Karl-Jesko von Puttkamer, Press Officer Heinz Lorenz, and Göring's Air Force liaison officer with *FHQ* Gen. Karl Bodenschatz (in front of Lorenz), Foreign Office adjutant Ambassador Walter Hewel, unknown Army officer, aide *SS* Gen. Julius Schaub (behind Jodl's cap), *SS* aide Max Wünsche (behind Schaub), Himmler's *SS* liaison with *FHQ* Maj. Gen. Karl Wolff, physician Dr. Theodor Morell, and *SS* aide Hans-Georg Schulze. (HHA)

Hitler's G-4 seen driving through the German village of Rodert near his *FHQ Felsennest* in 1940. According to *After the Battle* in 1977, the lady in the apron with the camera at left—Frau Maria Bresgn—still lived in the same village 37 years later. Note that all the lamp covers are in place and the license plate is also covered, but—oddly—the *Führerstandarte* is affixed on the right mudguard—a strange contradiction of security! The only car occupants visible here are adjutant Julius Schaub at the right rear and *SS* valet Heinz Linge standing at the left rear. (HHA)

According to *After the Battle,* Friday, 17 May, Bastogne (Belgium). "A detachment of the *FBB* under 1st Lt. Struck (comprising Hitler's six-wheeled Mercedes-Benz (G-4), four other six-wheelers for the escort, and one reserve car) met Hitler's party at the airfield and drove him to Army Group A headquarters at #3 Avenue de la Gare." The date marked the very first Front Group visit by Hitler in his G-4 on the new Western Front. Bastogne itself would not become famous until over four years later, during the epochal Battle of the Bulge, known as the Rundstedt Offensive in the United Kingdom. Seen here standing from left to right are Heinz Linge, Hitler, Engel, and Schaub, with Erich Kempka driving. (HHA)

Stated *After the Battle,* "By the time Hitler came for another conference, the headquarters had moved to Charleville-Mezieres. On Friday, May 24th, a guard party from the *FBB* under Capt. von Blomberg escorted Hitler from the airdrome to von Rundstedt's HQ in Blairon House on Avenue Georges Corneau [seen here]." (HHA)

According to my 1999 book *Mercedes-Bnez Parade and Staff Cars of the Third Reich,* "This was Hitler's first trip to the Western Front from his Belgian *FHQ* on May 17, 1940, to visit Gen. Gerd von Rundstedt's command at Bastogne, head of Army group A. Here, from left to right, are seen in the G-4 Hitler, *SS* valet Heinz Linge, Army adjutant Capt. Gerhard Engel, Gen. von Rundstedt (promoted field marshal following this successful campaign), and *Führer* adjutant *SS* Gen. Julius Schaub. Note that not a single *SS* or RSD man is visible, as Hitler evidently felt secure among his own troops, who seem happy to see him. The car is painted *Wehrmacht* gray, and all lamp covers are in place, as this was the first field trip in the seventh day of the campaign and the Belgian roads were unsafe due to land mines." Note, also, the small lamp at the center of the honeycomb radiator between the two covered headlamps. (HHA)

The cover painting by artist George A. Campbell of Hitler leaving von Rundstedt's Army Group A headquarters at Bastogne, Belgium, from *After the Battle's* 1991 book *Blitzkrieg in the West: Then and Now*. Seen here are Hitler giving his famous backhanded, casual, Nazi salute and *SS* chauffeur Erich Kempka at the wheel, with Capt. Engel (left) and Schaub (right) standing up behind them. *(ATB.)*

Stated *After the Battle's Hitler on the Western Front* by Jean-Paul Pallud: "Entering Brussels (Belgium) from the east, the (G-4) motorcade arrives at the Cinquantenaire Arch, a monument built to commemorate the 50th anniversary of the founding of Belgium in 1831. From the war diary of the *FHQu* Kommandantur, we know the composition of the *FBB* convoy which toured Brussels on June 1, 1940. The first echelon comprised five motorcars, including one for Hitler, another for Keitel, one containing the ADCs, and two with security guards. The second echelon formed the motorcycle platoon under 1st Lt. Bock, the Flak platoon under 1st Lt. Rossmann, with one vehicle in reserve. Following in the third echelon under 1st Lt. Neumann were the communications team, an armored car for reconnaissance, the field kitchen, and a vehicle carrying supplies and luggage." (HHA)

Continues Pallud: "Instead of driving directly to Ghent, Hitler's motorcade made a detour north to have a look at the bridges blown by the Belgians over the Willebroek Canal. There had been a battle at Kapelle-op-den-Bos on May 17, 1940, when the Belgians sent two of their ACG 1 light tanks to cover the demolished bridges and try to stop the Germans from crossing the canal." (HHA)

States Pallud: "After exposing 10 more frames, the party reached the Grand Place, which is the main square in Brussels. This shot was taken on the western side as Hitler's car was about to drive into Rue de Marche au Charbon. Nothing has changed (1991) in the historical center of Brussels, always a popular tourist destination...." (HHA)

Notes Pallud: "While Hitler and his generals were absorbed in yet another conference—this time with Col. Gen. (Walter) von Reichenau, the 6th Army commander, and his staff at Bissegem airfield—their aides were able to relax outside. (Reich Photo Reporter Prof.) Heinrich Hoffmann (center) is in conversation with some SS men," members of both the *Führer's* SS/RSD/FBB security escort. (HHA)

Asserts Pallud: "The convoy then crossed Ypres on its way to Langemark, 10 kilometers to the north. Here, they pass the partly rebuilt Cloth Hall. This great building had been destroyed in 1915 during month-long German artillery barrages." Note, too, the license plate. (HHA)

An *SS* security guard (center) strides past an impressive line-up of Gray Column G-4s, with machine guns mounted. Stated Pallud: "The *Führer's* party ...stopped for a visit to Mt. Kemmel a strategic hill that had been taken by the Germans in April 1918." Hitler and his entourage also visited the nearby Belvedere café, still there in 1991. (HHA)

Notes Pallud: "On the evening of Saturday, June 1st instead of driving directly to the *FHQ* Chateau de Brigode at (Annapes), where he was to spend the night. Hitler chose instead to backtrack and tour the center of Lille (France), where he had been billeted in October 1914. Jean-Paul: 'Studying the exposures of Hoffmann Roll 5045, frame by frame, I followed the route of the convoy as it proceeded along Place du Theatre, Rue Faidherbe, Place de la Gare, Rue de Tournai…' A few townspeople and some German soldiers gathered in front of the railway station were surprised as Hitler passed them by.'" (HHA)

Says Pallud: "Before leaving the Canadian Memorial Park (at Vimy Ridge) Hitler stopped to walk over that part of the old front line which had been preserved just as it had been left in 1918, complete with trenches and craters. The party then set off for the French Memorial and Cemetery at Notre Dame de Lorette, Hitler sitting beside his chauffeur, SS Maj. Kempka." Note, also, the deep tread on the mounted tire at left! (HHA)

From my 1999 book *Mercedes-Benz Parade and Staff Cars of the Third Reich*: "A close-up of Hitler's G-4 in the West, Spring 1940, showing a smiling Kempka at the wheel and an equally affable *Führer* at his right, pleased by the reception given him by the German Army troops surrounding his car….Standing behind in the car is *Wehrmacht* (chief) adjutant Col. Rudolf Schmundt….This view presents a good view of the width of the searchlight covers and the inset door frame handles (at center.) Note that the sun visors are in the up position." (HHA)

Hitler's convoy at Arras, France. States Pallud: "By the time Hitler visited Arras in June 1940, the beautiful Hotel de Ville/City Hall on the Place des Heros had been rebuilt in the original style of the 15th and 16th Centuries." (HHA)

Notes Pallud: "Hitler's motorcade turned left in front of the railway station, heading northeastwards in the direction of Douai [WWI site of an airdrome used by Baron Manfred von Richtofen's famed *Flying Circus*]. Whether German troops had been warned in advance of the *Führer's* visit, we do not know, but many were out on the street to cheer him as he passed by." (HHA)

Asserts Pallud: "After reaching Douai, the convoy continued eastwards in the direction of Bouchain, where they were to meet with General of Artillery Heitz, the commander of the 8th Army Corps. Jean-Paul: 'I found that this picture had been taken at the level crossing at Sin-le-Noble about two kilometers east of Douai. As can be seen in the picture, the Germans had not evacuated people along the roads followed by the convoy (unlike some of the other places where Hitler was to stop for a walkabout). Nevertheless, guards were posted at crossroads and other spots considered vulnerable." (HHA)

Not a G-4 but…I incorrectly captioned this photo thus in my 1999 Mercedes book: "Himmler drives an open Cabriolet tourer at his headquarters in East Prussia, during the first stage of the Russian campaign—and the Holocaust, 1941. Next to the *ReichsFührer* is Dr. (Hans Heinrich) Lammers, while Karl Wolff sits at back on the right and an *SS* orderly with a camera on the left." I now believe that Jean-Paul Pallud's 2002 caption is more accurate, and thus I include it here as a correction: "It would appear from the photographic evidence that Himmler and Lammers had traveled together from (*FHQ*) *Wolfsschlucht* and, contrary to what has always been written, it was while Hitler was on his way *to* Rethondes that he had stopped at Laon and Urcel, not on the return journey. The analysis of Hoffmann's negatives (film rolls 5070 and 5072) clearly proves the point." Thus, this is France 1940, and *not* East Prussia 1941. In addition, I now also believe that the man with the camera is probably the bodyguard of *RFSS* Himmler—Josef Kiermaier—and *not* an orderly. (HHA)

Awaiting the arrival of the *Führer's* G-4 at Compiegne, Rethondes, France, to deliver the armistice terms to the defeated French on June 21, 1940. Göring and von Below (hidden by his service chief here) stride past a parked G-4. In the rear is the French 1918 victory memorial, covered with the Reich War Flag designed by Prof. Albert Speer in 1935. (Photo by Helmuth Kurth, the Hermann Göring Albums, LC, Wash., DC.)

Awaiting Hitler's arrival at Rethondes, France, at the Compiegne clearing are from left to right: German Army Commander-in-Chief Col. Gen. Walther von Brauchitsch (wearing riding spurs on his boots), Foreign Minister Joachim von Ribbentrop (facing the camera lens), and Göring, clutching his *Luftwaffe* field marshal's ornate dress baton behind his back, June 21, 1940. Today, the actual baton is on display at the United States Army Infantry School Museum at Ft. Benning, GA, where the present author was an Officer Candidate during 1966. (Photo by Helmuth Kurth, HGA, LC, Wash., DC.)

A quartet of top Nazis amid parked Mercedes at Compiegne clearing at Rethondes, France, on June 21, 1940. From left to right are: (center) *RFSS* Heinrich Himmler; *SS* Maj. Gen. Karl Wolff, Himmler's deputy; Foreign Minister Joachim von Ribbentrop; and Reich Chancellery chief Dr. Hans Heinrich Lammers. Most likely, this was shot *after* the trip seen in the top left picture on page 148, and thus on the very same day. (Photograph from the Joachim von Ribbentrop Albums, USNA, College Park, MD/USA.)

The *Führer's* arrival at Compiegne, June 21, 1940, as driver Kempka turns his head to the right. Göring's head is seen just over the top of the hood, and an *SS* officer is to his right, below the French monument. (HHA)

An excellent color view of the *Führer's* arrival at Compiegne, June 21, 1940, with his G-4 in the foreground. Seen from left to right are Navy Grand Adm. Dr. Erich Raeder with ornate baton, Nazi Party Deputy *Führer* Rudolf Hess, von Brauchitsch (back to camera), and Göring. (Walter Frentz)

From my 1999 work: "Martin Bormann (1900-45) was named a *Reichsleiter* on Oct. 10, 1933, and prior to that—on July 1st—was made Chief of Staff to Hitler's Deputy *Führer*, Rudolf Hess. In that capacity he became Hess' liaison officer to Hitler at his various residences…Here, Bormann is in the right front passenger seat of a G-4 in France in 1940, looking glum and wearing motoring goggles on his cap visor." (Walter Frentz)

Martin Bormann (facing camera), was the Nazi who benefited most from the flight of Rudolf Hess to Scotland on May 10, 1941. Seen here with his *SS* chauffeur in German-occupied France in 1940, Bormann was about to prepare the way for Hitler's one and only sightseeing tour of Paris on June 23, 1940. (Previously-unpublished photo from the Heinrich Hoffmann Albums, USNA, College Park, MD/USA.)

"The end of the trip by G-4, following an exciting three hours." (HHA)

#236

#237

As I noted in 1999: "Research indicates that these three photos of a trip to Paris are not likely to be the trip on June 23, 1940, but of a separate trip either before, during, or after that famous trip of the *Führer's*. The cars appear alone, and not with the rest of the *Führerkolonne*...According to (the late) Robert M. Snibbe—founder of the Napoleonic Society of America—the scene in **#236** is most likely the French Ministry of Marine (Navy) on the Place de la Concorde. From left to right is Nazi *Gauleiter/Regional Leader* of Münich Adolf Wagner, Martin Bormann in the open door, *SS* Dr. Karl Brandt leaning over the car seat, with *Führer* adjutant Julius Schaub standing on the running board on the driver's side. One assumes that the man in the dark coat at right is French, surveying his country's conquerors. Bormann wears his ever-present motoring goggles. Mr. Snibbe of the NSA feels that **#237** is at the Palace of Versailles, the scene of the 1871 Proclamation of the German Empire after the Prussian victory over the French, and the 1919 Treaty of Versailles that ended World War I and helped cause World War II. Happy Nazis are in the G-4 that we see here. The third view, **#238**, Snibbe feels, is of the Palace of Versailles, from the top of a hill there, with the Statue of Louis XIV in the distance. Martin Bormann stands in the center in high boots, hands on hips, the two G-4s behind him." (HHA)

#238

"Adolf Hitler made a sole visit to the surrendered French capital, Paris, on June 23, 1940, and this is how the city looked through his windshield.The scene is taken from behind his head, with Kempka's right hand on the steering wheel at left." (HHA)

The *Führer* (white raincoat) and entourage, departure, Le Bourget airport Paris, June 23, 1940. At far left is sculptor Dr. Breker, with Gen. Jodl next, then two unidentified men, and next Prof. Albert Speer, looking away to his left, and Gen. Keitel (hands clasped behind his back). Note the waiting two G-4s at center rear. There were five in all. "According to Hitler's pilot, Hans Baur, the *Führer's* Government Flight landed at Le Bourget at 5 AM. 'Because Hitler wanted to get his visit over and done with before the Parisians were on the streets, I went along with him on his tour through the town. Workmen were tramping along going to the factories; the street sweepers were just starting their jobs; and the concierges were beginning to open up the front doors.'" The start and finish of the Paris tour…as all accounts agree, was Le Bourget airfield. (HHA)

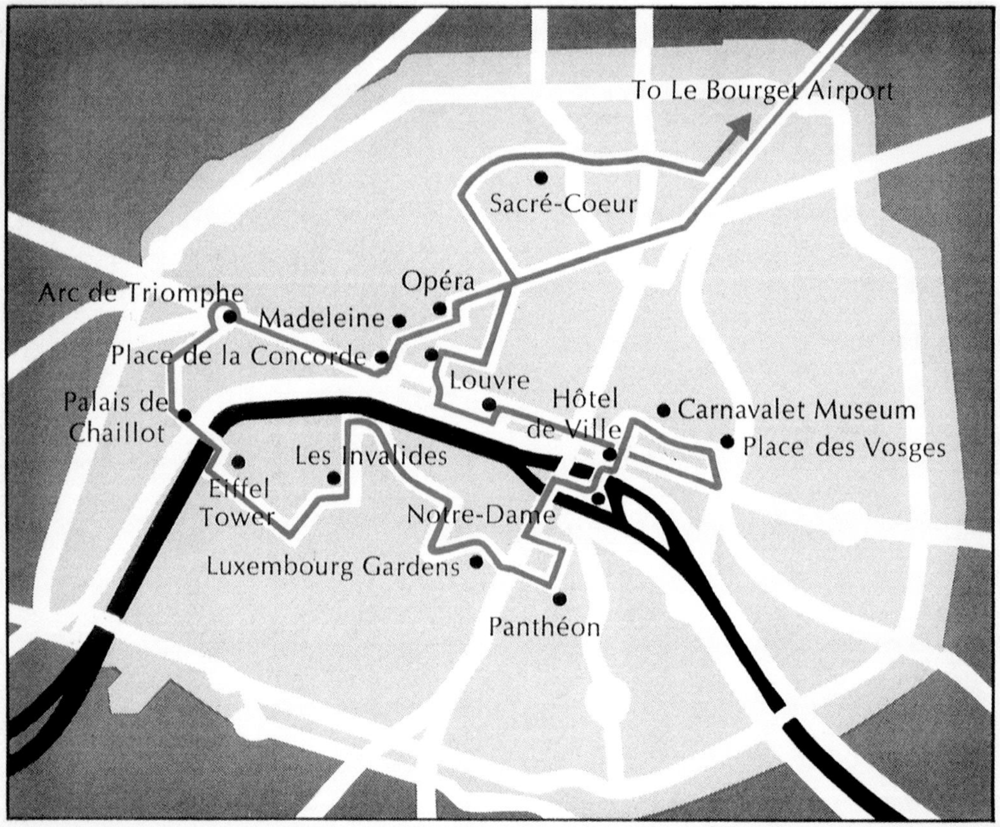

HITLER'S PARIS ITINERARY

"As seen on the map, according to Baur, 'From the airfield, we drove along the Champs Elysees to the Arc de Triomphe and the grave of the Unknown Soldier. Then we visited the Louvre, the Trocadero, the Eiffel Tower, the Paris Opera, and, finally, the Invalides, where Hitler was particularly interested in the Tomb of Napoleon. By 6 O'clock, we were back again on the airfield…This one-hour time-frame seems improbable when one consults the map!"

States Jean-Paul Pallud: "The convoy crossed the Place de l'Etoile, turning around the Arc de Triomphe. From his studies of plans of the city, Hitler knew Paris quite well, and he claimed that he would be able to find his way about the streets and monuments without a guide." Note the car pennant at lower left on the mudguard. Noted Dr. Speer: "Hitler as usual sat in the front seat beside the chauffeur, Breker and I on the jump seats behind him, while Giesler and the adjutants occupied the rear seats…We drove through the extensive suburbs directly to the Opera…It was Hitler's favorite, and the first thing he wanted to see. There, at 6 AM, he posed for photos, shocking the French newspaper vendors surprised to see him. From there, it was on to the Madeleine," a church built in 1806, Napoleon's Temple of the Grande Armee, which had then just defeated Prussia. (HHA)

Leaving the Place de la Concorde about 6 AM, with Hitler standing up in the lead G-4 at right. Note the still photographer in the follow–up car at right and—above him—newsreel lensman Walter Frentz standing to cover Hitler's trip at far right. In the *Führer's* car up ahead, Breker (left) is pointing, while Giesler is looking straight back. Notes author Frederic Spotts in his excellent 2003 work *Hitler and the Power of Aesthetics*, "Breker had spent many years in Paris; his Francophilia did not diminish his pleasure in showing Hitler around a defeated France." (HHA)

Above left: A good side view of the *Führer's* G-4 as it pulls up to the curb at the Madeleine in Paris, June 23, 1940. In this view, Hitler rides in the right front seat next to chauffeur *SS* Maj. Erich Kempka, as he generally did. Note also that Arno Breker sits on the left mid-car jump seat, next to Dr. Albert Speer. Note the foot hole over the top of the rear wheels on the side, and the luggage compartment at the rear with its insignia. Adds Jean-Paul Pallud: "Two architects—Albert Speer and Hermann Giesler—accompanied Hitler for his long-awaited visit to Paris. Also present on this lightning tour were some of his normal entourage like Keitel, Brückner, Schaub, (Dr. Otto) Dietrich, Bodenschatz, Schmundt, and Engel. The second stop of the tour was at the Church of La Madeleine. On the other side of the Seine River, another halt at Les Invalides was to contemplate the Tomb of Napoleon." Prof. Speer said in 1970 that the *Führer's* Parisian tour took three hours, and this author is inclined to accept that figure rather than Baur's one hour. He recalled: "Three large Mercedes sedans stood waiting at about 5:30 AM." (HHA)

States Pallud: "Hitler's car behind the Opera in Rue Gluck—a still from the cine-film....He had decided not to order a massive parade in Paris" as he told Prof. Speer: 'I am not in the mood for a victory parade. We're not at the end yet.'" As for the visit to Paris, "Uniforms were provided for the artists so that they befitted the occasion. They took off for Le Bourget from Gros Caillou airfield near *FHQ Wolfsschlücht* at Bruly-de-Pesche, a small village in the Gontrieux Forest in southern Belgium." At Le Bourget, asserts Pallud: "The 10-car convoy moved off, driving six kilometers down the N2 to enter the city at Port de la Villette." (Walter Frentz)

States Pallud: "Another cine-frame of the convoy proceeding south on Rue Royale after visiting the Madeleine...As the first thing Hitler wanted to see was the Opera House, the route ran via the Rue de Flandre and Rue La Fayette. Here, the cine-cameraman (Frentz) was in action for the first time, filming Hitler's car behind the Opera in Rue Gluck...After the group left the Opera House, the convoy continued via the Boulevard des Capucines to the Madeleine...Moving south on Rue Royale, the cine-film recorded the scene as the cars reached the Place de la Concorde, and turned right to rise up the 2 kilometer-long Avenue des Champs Elysees. At this point, Hitler ordered the cars to stop so that he could fully appreciate the magnificent view up to the Arc de Triomphe." (Walter Frentz)

Notes Pallud: "Hitler's (G-4) Mercedes pulls up at the Trocadero—a cine-still," but parked facing the wrong way! It was then that Hitler and his entourage viewed the Eiffel Tower, erected in the very year of the *Führer's* birth, 1889. Prior to that, "The cars ascended the hill, circuited the Etoile and proceeded down Avenue Foch. Reaching the Avenue Poincare, the cavalcade turned left to the Place du Trocadero [as seen here]. After returning to the cars, the journey continued by crossing the Seine (River) via the Pont d'Iena [the battle in which the Prussians had been defeated by the French in 1806], past the Eiffel Tower and the deserted Parc du Champ de Mars for a stop outside the *Ecole Militaire/Military School*." (Walter Frentz)

"Approaching the Arc de Triomphe," states *Time-Life Books*, "As seen from Gen. Keitel's car," as I noted in 1999, "just behind the first group containing Hitler's car and escort." Resumes Pallud about the overall route, "The convoy then drove slowly to the Odeon Theater and down the Boulevard St. Michel and Rue Soufflot to the Pantheon, built over the grave of St. Genevieve, the patron saint of Paris...With the tour half completed, Breker records that Hitler wanted to get an impression of the surroundings in which he, himself, had lived and worked. The journey therefore continued south to the Boulevard Montparnase to the Café Closeirie des Lilas where Breker showed Hitler the fantastic plastic art 'Rudes' by Marshal Ney." (HHA)

"Beside the statue of Marshal Joffre," states Pallud of this cine-film shot. "Continuing to the Place Vauban, Hitler entered the Dome des Invalides to see the Tomb of Napoleon. Changing his heavy leather coat for a lighter one, he stood for a long time contemplating the great marble tomb...The party moved through the Church of St. Louis (behind the Dome) to the courtyard of the Hotel des Invalides, where the cars were waiting. The next part of the tour was not photographed by Hoffmann, but ran via the Quai d'Orsay [the French Foreign Ministry], Chamber of Deputies [the lower house of the French Parliament], across the Rue de Lille and along the Boulevard St. Germain. It continued past the French War Ministry and the Rue Bonaparte to St. Sulpice Church and the Palace of Luxembourg." (Walter Frentz)

A color view of Hitler's G-4 leaving the Place de la Concorde in Paris on June 23, 1940, with the *Führer* seen standing in his car at left, and Frentz photographing the scene with his motion picture camera at top right, plus the still photographer at lower right. In 1973, when asked if he had ever seen Hitler, a German painter born in 1921 answered, "In 1943 in Paris (sic). Seeing Hitler didn't impress me at all at the time; I already hated him. As he was driving through Paris in his car, you got the impression of a man who is hunted, but who still manifests power, even at the end of his life. He was surrounded by alert officers and scout cars, things like that. He made anything but the impression of a man who was the ruler of Europe. He just roared through like that. It wasn't an official visit, either, but more like a kind of check." (HHA)

As I noted in 1999: "The Gray Column of G-4s approaches the Arc de Triomphe, as seen from just behind Gen. Keitel's head in his car." Continues the Pallud account of the overall Parisian tour, "Then, retracing their route back along the Boulevard St. Michel—being saluted by some French policemen on the way (to which Hitler replied)—they passed the Square de Cluny. Pointing to a dome on the right-hand side of the street, Hitler asked Breker if this was the Tribunal of the Chamber of Commerce. Breker remembers that he said no, and that he believed it to be the dome of the Insitute of France. When they passed the building, Hitler said, amused, 'Look what it says, Chamber of Commerce.' Breker comments that Hitler had really prepared himself well for this visit so that he was able to compete quite well using his theoretical knowledge against an old Parisian!" (HHA)

Hitler's party has left its G-4—parked the wrong way at the Trocadero—and walks from it toward the Eiffel Tower in the distance, as viewed from the rear of their own perspective. From left to right: Capt. Engel, Dr. Speer, Hitler, and Prof. Breker. The 984-foot structure was once the world's tallest. This picture and others shocked the world into taking Hitler seriously at last. Until then, he had seemed to many a harmless figure of ridicule, a shouting, gesticulating fool. In his postwar memoirs, Prof. Breker recalled the following incident that took place on the tour: "Suddenly, in the quiet of the morning, we heard the hoarse call of a newspaper salesman coming nearer and nearer. He turned into the Rue de Rivoli, saw the convoy of cars and jumped forward. He offered us a newspaper in his stretched out hand. Suddenly, he recognized Hitler. The call '*Le Matin/Morning!*' died on his lips, he stared, and then—panic-stricken—dropped all his newspapers and ran to the safety of the nearest open doorway. Barely a hundred yards further on—at the corner of the Rue des Halles—stood a small group of market women, stout, self-assured, and full of temperament. Reaching them, the biggest of the women suddenly stretched out her arms and pointed to Hitler, and, full of enthusiasm, she shouted, 'It's him It's him!'—whereupon the group dispersed." (HHA)

As Hitler's G-4 (left) prepares to pass under the Eiffel Tower, note the German motorcyclist who goes on ahead (right). Continues the Pallud account of the tour: "The next stop was at the Palace of Justice, where they saw the St. Chappelle, the only part of the old French castle to be spared the fire which destroyed it in the 17th Century. Breker says that, having got into a Gothic mood, they then visited the highlight of any Paris tour, the nearby Notre Dame. Afterwards, crossing from the Ile de la Cite, via the Pont d'Arcole, they stopped at the *Hotel de Voille/City Hall*. Then, diverting eastward, they visited the Carnavelt Museum, passing thence via the Place des Vosges, to the Rue de Rivoli and LesHalles, the market center of Paris. Breker says there were few people about, a sign that the city had been evacuated." (HHA)

The *Führer*—now having replaced the heavier leather overcoat with this white and lighter raincoat—and his entourage standing on the heights of Montmartre at the Church of *Sacre Coeur* (*Sacred Heart*) overlooking Paris, June 23, 1940. The magnificent, panoramic view presented of the city at their feet provided the Nazi conquerors with a fitting end to their once-in-a-lifetime tour. The church, ironically, had been built for the loss of the war of 1870 to the Prussians, and now here the Germans were, 70 years later! From left to right are Army Col. Hans Speidel (top aide to Field Marshal Rommel in 1944 and postwar NATO commander-in-chief during 1957-63), Hitler, Martin Bormann, Dr. Speer, architect (and chief Speer rival) Prof. Hermann Giesler (behind Speer), sculptor Prof. Arno Breker, *SS* ordnance adjutant 1st Lt. Max Wünsche, and *SA* adjutant Wilhelm Brückner (back to camera). The left side G-4 handrail is seen in the lower right-hand corner of the photo. Before the war, Speidel had been a captain and assistant military attaché in Paris, and thus was sent for by Gen. Fedor von Bock on June 14, 1940, to enter the city and prepare the way: first for him, and then later for the *Führer.* He recalled: "I came through Le Bourget by myself, while ahead of me were only some armored cars." In 1963, when Gen. Charles de Gaulle—then President of France—threw NATO out of his country, then-Gen. Speidel was sent packing a second time, the first having been in 1944. In 1940 de Gaulle had been but a defeated French armored division commander. Indeed, the wheel of fate had turned full circle for *both* soldiers! (HHA)

"A Dictator's Dream Tour: Adolf Hitler with his escort on the heights of Montmarte" is how *Time-Life Books' World War II* series captioned this panoramic photograph. The scene is on the famous Esplanade at Sacre Coeur, with Hitler clutching closed the front of his white raincoat and heading for his G-4, parked at the curb at the left, as the rest of his entourage scurries for their vehicles as well. The car at the far right is that of Gen. Wilhelm Keitel, his *OKW* mudguard pennant clearly visible. The wrought-iron gate at the far right belongs to the steps leading up to the church. The fence in the distance on the heights still stands. At the far left, Prof. Breker is about to enter Hitler's G-4 from the far side, followed by Dr. Giesler, then Gen. Brückner, and lastly Dr. Dietrich. Walking behind Hitler in a line-up in this order are Capt. Gerhard Engel, *SS* Gen. Julius Schaub, Gen. Keitel, Gen. Karl Bodenschatz (to the left), and lastly *SS* 1st Lt. Wünsche (further left). Martin Bormann is at the right of Capt. Engel. At the very center of the picture—back to camera, standing at the fence—is the late cinema photographer Walter Frentz, taking in the scenic view of Paris thus afforded via his newsreel motion picture camera. According to French author Jean-Paul Pallud, the time is exactly 8:15 AM, June 23, 1940. Adds *After the Battle*: "Hitler's stop at the Basilica du Sacre Coeur was the last stop of his three-hour tour. 'From up there,' says Breker, 'the panorama of the city—now plunged into radiant sunshine—resembled an enormous tapestry with beautiful patterns whose most eminent features stood out.' 'Many churchgoers recognized Hitler,' says Speer, 'but ignored him.'...By 8:15 AM, the tour was over, and the party returned to Le Bourget...Hitler turned to Albert Speer: 'It was the dream of my life to see Paris. I cannot say how happy I am to have that dream fulfilled today.' 'For a moment,' Speer says, 'I felt something like pity for him: three hours in Paris, the one and only time he was to see it, made him happy when he stood at the height of his triumphs.'...The route *to* Montmartre had been thus: 'Continuing along the Rue de Rivoli, the Louvre was quickly visible on the left...continued past the Opera, along the Rue de la Chausee d'Anrin to Place de Clichy and on to Pigalle and Montmartre. From there it ran via the roundabout route, around the many small streets, necessary to reach the Basilica du Sacre Coeur, the final stop.'" (HHA)

Far left: According to *After the Battle*: "With Max Amann and Ernst Schmidt, two of his old comrades from (WWI Bavarian) Infantry Regiment 16, having joined his regular group. On the morning of Tuesday, June 25, 1940, Hitler left *FHQ Wolfsschlucht/Wolf's Gorge* for the Champagne area of France on his own personal battlefield tour. At Laon, he drove up to the top of the hill on which the town is built to visit the cathedral [seen here, with G-4 parked at right, and Front Group motorcycles at left]. His entourage waited outside as Hitler entered the cathedral with Schmidt and Amann. Amann, who had been Hitler's company sergeant in WWI, had been a member of the Nazi Party from the beginning, and in 1940 was director of Eher Verlag, the Party's publishing house." (HHA)

Left: "The front of the cathedral in Reims," states *ATB*, "was still hidden behind sandbags piled up by the French to protect the 13th Century building from being damaged in the fighting. Reims had fallen into German hands on June 10, 1940." Continues Ludwig Kosche: "A very few G-4s were armored, and had removable windows with bullet proof glass 30mm thick. The G-4 which Hitler used for his trip to the *City of Light*—he used other G-4s as well—featured grips on both sides of the windscreen, but a second G-4 in his motorcade was also so equipped. Apparently, the same G-4s can also be seen in photographs taken when Hitler entered Warsaw on Oct. 5, 1939. The available photographic evidence indicates that there were no other G-4s with this particular characteristic, and one of these automobiles has survived! The applicable Daimler-Benz order is given as 340 837, with that for the engine being 440 875, and for the body 200 663. The vehicle was picked up from the factory on Aug. 28, 1939, and the manufacturer recorded the *Besteller/orderer* as the 'Administration Obersalzberg for the *Führer* and Reich Chancellor, Invoice: Administration Obersalzberg.'" (HHA)

States *ATB*, "Returning to Laon (the hilly city is visible in the background), Hitler and company turn southwards in the direction of Reims [where Col. Gen. Alfred Jodl would surrender to the Western Allies on May 7, 1945]. Near Festieux, about 10 kilometers south of Laon, they passed a disabled (French) Panhard armored car and the lonely grave of its crew. According to the late German car expert and author Ludwig Kosche, 'When Hitler visited Paris on (Sunday) June 23, 1940, he used his motor convoy, consisting of five Mercedes-Benz G-4s. These six-wheelers were designed for cross-country travel, and could seat up to seven people. The engine specifications are: straight eight (cylinders), without compressor, maximum (depending upon the model) piston displacement 5401 ccm, power output 115 hp, and top speed 42 mph.'" (HHA)

Says *ATB*, "On the second day of the battlefield tour—Wednesday, June 26th—the convoy drove into Fournes-en-Weppes and halted in front of the village butcher's shop. Like any ex-serviceman, Hitler was delighted to have returned to the house where he was billeted in 1916. Its location must have been researched earlier, as a notice had already been put in the shop window to signify its historical importance. This fact was later cast in stone when a large marble plaque identifying the building as the location of Hitler's 1916 billet was fixed to the façade in April 1942 (at) # 966 Rue Faidherbe, Fournes-en-Weppes, June 2002. Jean-Paul (Pallud): 'I found that the shop was now closed with the window bricked up but, in between the two windows of the first floor, the four pins on which the plaque once hung, were still to be seen. The plaque was broken when it was removed in 1944, but the pieces were saved and are now on display in the Fromelles Museum.' The inscription reads: 'In these quarters in 1916 lived our *Führer/Leader* Adolf Hitler as a soldier of the Bavarian Infantry Regiment List. Technical Department, Apr. 20, 1942,' for Hitler's 53rd birthday." (Photo by Peter Thompson, courtesy *ATB.)*

Notes Pallud: "To retrace his own footsteps of over two decades earlier, Hitler (center) then directed the convoy to the sector to the west where his regiment had been stationed from October 1917. *Sonderführer* Walter Frentz, the *FHQ* motion picture cameraman, can be seen at work while Hitler searches for a clue as to where he had been billeted some 22 years before." On Tuesday, June 25, 1940, "Hitler left *(FHQ)* Bruly-de-Peche at 9AM for the battlefields in Champagne. Unfortunately, there is nothing in the *FHQu* war diary to trace the precise route they followed, but five rolls of film taken by Hoffmann and his photographers (5078, 5079, 5080, 5081, and 5108) have enabled me to pinpoint salient points where they stopped. Traveling via Montcornet, the party first halted at Laon, where they visited the cathedral. They then drove out of the city to the west to visit Cerny-les-Bucy and the Fort de Laniscourt, Hitler obviously wanting to retrace his own footsteps when he was in this sector in 1917 and 1918." (HHA)

Attests Pallud: "The convoy has finally reached the remote Fort de Laniscourt along a field track and, followed by (Martin) Bormann, Hitler and Schmied went inside to inspect the central area of the fort [here]. The party leaves. Behind Schmidt (left) and Hitler (center) are, from left to right, Capt. von Below, Martin Bormann, and Max Amann (hidden by Hitler), and the tall figure of *SA* Lt. Gen. Wilhelm Brückner. In between Hitler and Brückner is *SS* Lt. Col. Dr. Karl Brandt. Continuing his journey south, Hitler next went to Montbavin, a small hilltop village, where he visited the church." Hidden behind Bormann is *SS* Maj. Gen. Julius Schaub. Considering Hitler's spreading middle-aged paunch as seen here, he would've done better to have worn a belt! Continues Ludgwig Kosche on Hitler's Parisian trip G-4: "It is necessary to note that in the same month (August 1939) another three G-4s were delivered to Münich, with the 'orderer' being 'the Administration Obersalzberg, c/o *Reichsleiter* M. Bormann (order numbers 309 803-309 805).' In view of these complications, it cannot be stated unequivocally that the surviving G-4 is the vehicle Hitler himself used in 1939 and 1940, but no doubt arises that it is one of the two G-4s with grips on both sides of the wind screen which can be seen in photographs of Hitler's motor convoy. This historic vehicle was traded from France to the United States a year ago, and is now part of the Blackhawk Classic Auto Collection in California." Schmidt was allegedly Hitler's homosexual lover during most of World War 1. (HHA)

Attests Pallud: "From Fournes, Hitler's tour continued north to Fromelles, where the front line had been in the summer of 1916. In July that year… the D141A road between Fournes and Fromelles…. Fromelles suffered badly in the First World War, and Hitler had difficulty recognizing where he had been. This picture of the tour group was taken at the southern entrance to the village in front of what was then the farm of Louis Equine…about midday." The *Führer* is seen about to enter his G-4 at the right. He then visited some bunkers in the Fromelles sector. (HHA)

Notes Pallud: "The party returned to their cars, where Schmidt was pictured watching Linge cleaning mud from Hitler's shoes [I think he means *boots* here instead]. A hundred meters or so off the picture to the right, Mrs. Adeline Fremaut was also observing the same scene, and it is to her recollection that we narrowed our search to the end of Rue de la Biette. She later recalled that she was digging in her garden that day when several German cars arrived, and men got out and walked into the field (See picture top right, page 150)." (HHA)

Says Pallud: "Having pinpointed Frame 25 on Roll 5090 as being taken at Toesbrugge, between Dunkirk and Poperinge, this scene was identified by him as being at Cappelle-la-Grande, just south of Dunkirk It seems that rain had suddenly started to fall and convoy had halted to raise their hoods/tops." (HHA)

Continues Pallud: "Leaving Fromelles—no doubt in high spirits having discovered their old bunker—the 1940 tour carried on to Aubers where Hitler stopped at the British Aubers Ridge cemetery. Driving southwards to La Bassee, the convoy then crossed the canal at the southern end of the town and seemingly turned westwards in the direction of Bethune…The photographer has now stopped his own vehicle by the side of the road to take a shot of Hitler's car passing by. The convoy was then moving northwards towards Dunkirk, possibly going via Hazebrouck, although there are no photos to prove it. It was not easy to trace the location where this picture was taken because there are hundreds of cafes in northern France sporting 'Motte Cordonier' advertising a local beer, and I received many false leads," he concludes. In this view, Hitler and Kempka are in front in their usual spots, while Max Amann is seen sitting in the mid-car jump seat behind, and to the rear of him are *SS* 1st Lt. Max Wünsche (left) and Capt. Gerhard Engel (right), seated on top of the trunk. (HHA)

"Having crossed Bergues, the German convoy then turned eastwards in the direction of Belgium. The rain must have stopped, because the journey had resumed with the tops down. This enabled the photographer to stand up while the car was on the move and take this shot of vehicles abandoned by the side of the road…driving along the D916A…at Rattekot, a small hamlet between Bergues and Rexpoede. The convoy continued along the D916A…The motorcade then crossed the Rhine (River) via a floating bridge, and returned to *FHQ Tannenberg/Pine Mountain*, traveling through Walkirch and Wolfach." Hitler had relocated his *FHQ* to *Tannenberg* in Germany's famed Black Forest area on Friday, June 28, 1940, and two days later conducted another battlefield tour, this time in the contested Alsace region that had been exchanged between Germany and France time and again since the Napoleonic Wars. "On the return journey, the party stopped by the Rhine near Breisach to inspect battered French casemates." (HHA)

Hitler's G-4 and Gray Column crossing a destroyed bridge in Alsace, as German Army *Pioneeren* (*Engineers*) stand at right as witnesses to history, while Capt. Gerhard Engel rides on the running board to *SS* driver Kempka's left. (HHA)

The *Führer's* G-4 near Schlettsstadt-Colmar, Alsace, in France on June 30, 1940, so that Hitler can apply the common touch with his soldiers at right, the scene photographed by the late *Luftwaffe* motion picture lensman Walter Frentz at center for the weekly German theater newsreels. (HHA)

From my 1993 book *Guarding the Führer: Sepp Dietrich, Johann Rattenhuber and the Protection of Adolf Hitler*: "Hans-Georg Schulze (center) was Hitler's *SS* ordnance officer from October 1939-August 1941, when he was killed in action serving in Russia…He had replaced Max Wünsche as ordnance officer…Schulze looking trim and dapper in France with Hitler (third from right) in France in 1940, is watched at far right by the man he replaced, Wünsche." Behind them all are the parked G-4 cars of the *Führerkolonne*. (Eva Braun Hitler Albums, USNA, College Park, MD/USA.)

From the same work: "A rare view of the Adjutants' G-4 in France, 1940, behind which sits German armed motorcycle escort troops. The occupants are Hoffmann in the middle (jump) seat, with Dr. Karl Brandt sitting on the back of the left middle seat. Sitting in the back at left is RSD chief Johann Rattenhuber, and at right is an unknown Party official." (HHA)

From my 1999 work *Mercedes-Benz Parade and Staff Cars of the Third Reich*: "The Odendorf airfield near *FHQ Felsennest*, where light planes are parked next to a small fleet of the *Führer's* G-4s, all with the tops down. It was here that Hitler's aircraft, a Junkers Ju-52, flew to Bastogne on May 17, 1940, to meet von Rundstedt. There, waiting, was his own armored G4 and five other Mercedes; two for the *FBK*, two more for the military entourage, and another kept in reserve, in case Hitler's car was either disabled by the enemy, or simply broke down. Few chances were taken during the *Führer's* travels, and difficulties were planned for in advance as much as possible." (HHA)

From the same work: "Hitler arrives at Brussels airfield in Belgium on June 1, 1940 to be met by Gen. Fedor von Bock, commander of Army Group B. Notes author Peter Hoffmann, 'Dozens of Air Force men practiced private photography,' as seen here. The procession visited both the 1940 battlefields and the World War I cemeteries of German dead from the Battles of Ypres and Langemarck, the latter where German students linked arms and walked into pointblank enemy machinegun fire. The night was spent at (*FHQ*) Chateau de Brigode [at Annapes]." (HHA)

Above: From the same source: "Warlord meets pooch in a typical Western Front roadside stop, as Hitler bends down to get a wet kiss, watched and photographed by members of his entourage. On June 2, 1940, the Gray Column toured the French areas of Avelin, Vimy, Arras, Douai (scene of von Richthohfen's World War I airfield), Bouchain, and Cambrai, from where Hitler once more boarded his Ju-52 aircraft for a trip to Charleville, where Gen. von Rundstedt reported once more to him. That night, Hitler flew back to *FHQ Felsennest*, arriving at 6:30 PM (See bottom picture, page 146)." (HHA)

Above left: States Dr. Peter Hoffmann in *Hitler's Personal Security*, "RSD detail during tour of the front with Hitler in Belgium, June 1-2, 1940 (from left): Paul Leciejewski, Karl Weckerling, Hans Kuffner, Josef Jorg, Peter Högl, Josef Hausner, and Franz Grill." Note, also, the small searchlight cover in place with the nighttime driving light emission slit running vertically at center. (HHA)

Left: From my 1999 work: "The G-4 in France in 1940, with all lamp covers affixed, the *Führerstandarte* in place on the right front mudguard and the Nazi Party pennant on the left front. Standing behind Hitler is *Wehrmacht* adjutant Col. Rudolf Schmundt. Standing outside the car just past the right front fender is *SS* bodyguard Karl Wilhelm Krause, wearing *Waffen/Armed SS* field gray overcoat, a pistol holster close at hand on his belt. RSD chief Johann Rattenhuber's face can be seen between the searchlight on the right side of the car and the handrail. At left are Reich Labor Service (RAD) men, and at center are two Hitler Youth (HJ) members in black uniforms. Note the open vents on the left-hand side of the engine cover. The fog lamp is also visible at bottom center." (HHA)

From the same work: "At von Ribbentrop's Foreign Ministry field headquarters in France in 1940... The two posted *Luftwaffe* sentries present arms as the *Führer* and his foreign Minister (right) exit the latter's HQ. Note the *Führer* Standard and covered headlamps on Hitler's G-4 Mercedes at left." (Joachim von Ribbentrop Albums, USNA, College Park, MD/USA.)

Hitler's Gray Column G-4 *SS*/RSD security at the ready on the Western Front, 1940. (HHA)

The *Führer's* Gray Column in Lille, France, June 1940, amidst "vestiges of street fighting," according to author Aaron L. Johnson's *Hitler's Military Headquarters*: "Hitler went with his entourage on a round trip through Lille and then to the Vimy heights, where he met with the commanding general of the 15th Army Corps (motorized), General of Infantry Hermann Hoth." (HHA)

Col. Schmundt (left) talks with the RSD security detail as the G-4 is refueled from the petrol tank at center, with globe, France, 1940. (HHA)

"On Christmas Day 1940, the *Führer* (left) made a surprise visit to JG26 at Abbeville (on the Channel coast). Here, Adolf Galland (right), Kommodore of JG26, replies to Hitler's speech," according to authors Col. Raymond F. Toliver and Trevor J. Constable in their 1990 work *Fighter General: The Life of Adolf Galland*. Note the *Führer's* parked G-4, with top up, seen through the window at left. (HHA)

General of the Fighters Adolf Galland (1911-96), as seen in a wartime portrait wearing Knight's Cross with Oak Leaves at the throat. (CER.)

A previously-unpublished photograph of German Reich Marshal Hermann Göring (left) and his *Luftwaffe* General of the Fighters in German-Occupied France, 1941. The *Reichsmarchall* carries his informal swagger stick baton in his right, missing since the war. Over his right shoulder can also be seen Col. Gen. Karl Bodenschatz, and at far right his own adjutant, Col. Bernd von Brauchitsch. (Hermann Göring Albums, Library of Congress, Wash., DC.)

Crystal City, VA/USA, 1987, from left to right: author Blaine Taylor, Capt. Heidi Horn-Galland, and the late Gen. Adolf Galland, known the world over to his legion of friends as simply "Dolfo." I was privileged to have been one of them, and conducted the last known published interview with the general in 1996. (Previously-unpublished photograph by Mrs. Sharon Mary Jones, Kingsville, MD/USA.)

According to author Aaron L. Johnson in *Hitler's Military Headquarters*: "On Apr. 26, 1941, Hitler made a tour in his (G-4) car to Graz via Marburg a.d. Douau and on the 27th Klagenfurt (photo above). He traveled then to Münich on the 28th, returning to Berlin." Linge is at the left rear seat. (HHA)

Hitler at the Atlantic Wall? Maybe, with Frentz behind him (see top right page 125). (HHA)

6

Eastern Front, Jakob Werlin, and the End 1941-1945

In his 1999 work *Hitler's Military Headquarters: Organization, Structures, Security, and Personnel*, author Aaron L. Johnson does a good job in providing the dates and locations of the *Führer's* wartime activities, possibly derived from Hitler's official daybook in the United States National Archives in Washington, D.C. I will only concern myself here with those dates that Hitler either did, or likely, used his G-4 cars.

He began the year 1941 on the Obersalzberg, in Bavaria, at *FHQ Berghof* (*Mountain Home*), and traveled to Salzburg to meet the *Duce* on 17 January. Back in Berlin on the 29th, he returned to Bavaria on 17 February. On 1 March he went to Vienna to include Bulgaria in the Tripartite Pact, returning to the *Berghof* on the 4th. On the 12th, he went to Linz, Austria, to celebrate the third anniversary of the *Anschluss*.

On the 16th, he was back in Berlin, then spent the entirety of the Balkan campaign from April 12-26, 1941, aboard *Special Train Amerika* at Mönichkirchen, Austria, in the Steiermark. During 26-28 April, Hitler visited Graz, Marburg, and Klagenfurt, and returned to the Reich capital once more.

On 5 May he was back on the *Obersalzberg*, making short trips by rail elsewhere. During June 24-November 7, 1941, Hitler was at *FHQ Wolfsschanze* (*Wolf's Lair*) at Rastenburg, East Prussia, directing the opening phase of his attack on the Soviet Union. On 28 August he and Mussolini took a famous G-4 car tour of the conquered Ukraine, and Hitler returned to East Prussia on the 29th.

On September 24, 1941, the *Führer* traveled to Borisow, in the USSR, to visit Army Group Center HQ and meet with Field Marshal Fedor von Bock. On 2 October, he gave a famous premature speech at the Berlin Sports Palace declaring that Russia had lost the war, and was in Münich 7 November to celebrate the 1923 Beer Hall *Putsch* (*Revolt*), returning to the *Wolf's Lair* by the 11th.

He was in Berlin for *Luftwaffe* funerals on the 21st and 28th, then headed east again. On December 2, 1941, Hitler was at Army Group South's headquarters at Poltava, USSR, to stave off defeat during the first winter crisis of the war, then returned to Berlin on the 9th to meet with the Grand Mufti of Jerusalem—and also to deal with Imperial Japan's sneak attack on Pearl Harbor, declaring war on the U.S. two days later. On the 16th, he was back east.

The year 1942 opened with the 12 February funeral of Dr. Fritz Todt at Berlin, then he returned to *FHQ* on the 15th. One month later, he returned to Berlin, and a month and a day later, was back at *Wolfsschanze*. During 16-24 April, he was at the *Berghof*, then met with Mussolini at *FHQ Castle Klessheim*, Salzburg, Austria, during April 29-30, 1942.

By 3 May, Hitler was back on the Eastern Front, making several short trips by air and rail during the period 21 May-26 June. From 17 July-31 October, Hitler relocated *FHQ* further east to Vinnitsa, Ukraine, at *Wehrwolf* (*Werwolf*)—not, perhaps, the best choice of name, given the famous movies by American actor Lon Chaney, Jr., of the 1930s!

On 28 September, Hitler spoke again at the Berlin Sports Palace, then returned to the Ukraine on 4 October, returning westward to *FHQ Wolf's Lair* on the 31st. He remained there until February 17, 1943, following the grim destruction of the German 6th Army in the Battle of Stalingrad, aside from short trips westward. During 7-23 November, Hitler was in Berlin, and returned to the *Wolf's Lair*.

Hitler opened campaign year 1943 on 17 February with a trip to see Field Marshal Erich von Manstein at Saporoszhe, in the USSR. From 21 February-13 March, Hitler spent his second segment at *FHQ Wehrwolf*, traveling again to see von Manstein on the 10th. On the 13th, he returned to *FHQ Wolf's Lair* from Ukraine, and during the next few months, Hitler made several short trips to and from there by both rail and air.

On July 19, 1943, Hitler went to Feltre, Italy, for an important conference with Mussolini, then returned to *Wehrwolf* on 27 August for a one-day meeting. Several such one-day trips followed that fall and winter.

The *Führer* began 1944 with several diplomatic meetings and military conferences at Berlin, Münich, and Salzburg, meeting with Field Marshals Rommel and von Rundstedt on June 17, 1944, at Margival, France, for his last trip on French soil of the war. During 18 June-14 July 1944, he was at the *Berghof*, excepting short trips, until he left there for the last time.

Beginning July 15, 1944, Hitler was back in East Prussia, and on the 20th there occurred the Army Bomb Plot blast that almost killed him. He left the *Wolf's Lair* for the final time on November 20, 1944, for Berlin, from which he again departed on 11 December to direct the Battle of the Bulge at *FHQ Adlerhorst* (*Eagle's Eyrie*) at Ziegenberg, Germany.

That fight lost by January 15, 1945, Hitler returned to Reich Capital Berlin, leaving it for a single day's trip to the Oder River front east of Berlin on March 11, 1945. Upon his return, the embattled Nazi *Führer* never left his capital again.

According to Prof. Peter Hoffmann in *Hitler's Personal Security*:

"Preparations for visits to the (Eastern) Front (from *Wolf's Lair*) were not made until July 17, 1941...On Aug. 4th, at 4 AM, he visited Army Group Center HQ at Borisow, to confer with von Bock, Guderian, and Hoth, returning on the same day.

"A complete Gray Column had been sent there, although there can be no doubt that the Army Group command could have found enough cars to take Hitler and his suite around. The same procedure was followed for a front tour to Berdichev on Aug. 6th to visit Army Group South (von Rundstedt)."

The fact of that matter, however, was simply that Hitler did not trust his own Army generals to neither arrest nor murder him on-site at their own headquarters, and thus relied on his own drivers, cars, and bodyguards whenever possible.

During August 25-28, 1941, the Italian Fascist *Duce* Benito Mussolini visited Hitler, both in East Prussia and in Occupied Ukraine, and in all cases "Hitler took his cars," according to Dr. Peter Hoffmann. Upon meeting von Rundstedt there, the two dictators:

"Were driven some 40 kilometers south to review an Italian division. Due to poor road conditions [as the *Führer's* HQ Diary recorded], the division had not arrived at the appointed place, and *Führer* and *Duce* traveled 20 kilometers further to meet the division.

"Then they returned to Uman, flew back to Krosno, and were driven back to *(FHQ) Installation Sud/South...*"

Dr. Hoffmann also reports:

"Motor traffic in Resticted Zone A (at Rastenburg) was restricted to cars of 'personalities from Reich ministers, Reich leaders, and field marshal up:' these and their drivers and other accompanying persons had to have valid passes.

"Supply cars and those of persons with officer rank living in Restricted Zone A could also be brought in. All others had to be left outside."

Finally, Dr. Peter Hoffmann reports these most interesting G-4 car statistics from Erich Kempka's postwar memoirs, *I Burned Hitler*:

"Kempka gives these measurements from memory: 45mm armor glass, 3.5-4mm specially hardened steel side-plates, -11mm floor plates tested and found safe against a 500g. charge of dynamite."

States the late Richard Raiber, MD, in his superb unpublished manuscript *Führer-Begleit-Battalion /The Front Gruppen/Groups*:

"The rapid progress of *Operation Barbarossa/Red Beard*...soon led to significant changes in organization and procedures which had been the earlier operational styles of the Front Groups and *Führer* Columns.

"The objectives of Hitler's front tours quickly became very widely separated in the enormous expanse behind the Russian front as well as increasingly more distant from the *FHQ*...than ever before.

"To cope with the problem, several Gray Columns were sent out and remained in Russia, each to separate areas from which one of them could be expected to drive to a captured Russian landing field and meet Hitler's aircraft upon orders received by radio. The Gray Columns of G-4s were known by the name of the SS officer in charge of each.

"A *Wehrmacht/Armed Forces* officer and a few men—not a full Front Group—from the *FBB* were attached to each Gray Column and were responsible for its tactical leadership...The complicated, interesting movements of Front Groups and Gray Columns in association with Benito Mussolini's visit to Hitler at the *Wolfsschanze* in late August 1941 are fully documented. An account of this event throws light on Front Group operations, and also opens a window on previously unreported details of the dictator's meeting.

"This would be the dictator's first visit to Hitler at the *Wolfsschanze*. Three Italian divisions had recently arrived in Uman, south of Kiev in the Ukraine, to join German Army Group South, and the Italian dictator had expressed a desire to pay a short visit to them...

"On Aug. 20, 1941, Gray Column Greiderer—then at Berdichev in the Ukraine—was ordered to drive 175 kilometers southeastward to Uman. The small group attached to it for tactical leadership was led by 1st Lt. Hans Bauer, a platoon leader in the *FBB's* 4th Tank Company...at Lemberg, Galicia [not to be confused with Hitler's longtime personal pilot of the same name].

"At 5 AM, Aug. 22nd, Front Group Bock...departed its quarters at the *Wolfsschanze* and headed southwestward across East Prussia, eastern Poland, and western Russia toward Uman.

"At about the same time, the Batallion's Motor Transport Column and its commanding officer, Lt. Siegmar Menard, left the *FHQ* and drove southwestward to an airfield at Terespol, Poland on the west bank of the Bug River, opposite Brest-Litovsk. Early on Aug. 23rd, Front Group Grundmann...followed the latter, and both arrived at Terespol that afternoon.

"On Aug. 24th, Front Group Schmidt...was directed to leave its base of operations at Bialystok, in western Byelorussia/White Russia, and drive to Terespol."

On August 26, 1941:

"Hitler and his guests were driven to the (*FHQ*) airfield, and were airborne at 7:50 AM to begin a 40-minute flight to Terespol. FG Grundmann had deployed at Terespol's landing field when the aircraft landed. It, as well as Lt. Menard's Motor Transport Column, had been placed under the command of Capt. Wulf Gasta, chief of the *FBB's* Flak Battery.

"Also waiting at the airfield were Field Marshals von Bock (Army Group Center), Gunther von Kluge (4th Army), and Albert Kesselring (2nd Air Fleet), who gave short reports. Hitler, the *Duce*, and the others were then driven in a *Führer* Column a few kilometers eastward, across the Bug River, to view the citadel at Brest.

"They used the G-4s supplied by Gray Column (GC) Schmidt…which had been shifted from Bialystok to Terespol for this mission. Returning to the landing field at Terespol, they lunched in tents erected by the Motor Transport Column.

"Reboarding their aircraft at 12:35 PM, they flew westward to land at 13:40 PM at Rostken Airfield, a few kilometers southeast of the Spirding See in East Prussia. One half of the Motorcycle Messenger Platoon, 2nd Company, was waiting with a GC at the airfield. Skirting the southern edge of the Spirding See, the *Führer* Column (FC) drove 25 kilometers westward, through the Johannisbourg Forest, to visit Reich Marshal Hermann Göring…at his temporary headquarters aboard *Sonderzug Asia/Special Train Asia*, parked on a siding near a tunnel, at Niedersee…

"Arriving at Niedersee at 2:10 PM, Hitler and his guests were served tea and given a report on recent *Luftwaffe* aerial operations in Russia by Lt. Gen. Hans Jeschonneck. At 4 PM, Hitler and the others departed northward in GC G-4s, and were back at *Wolfsschanze* by 5:50 PM.

"While Hitler, Mussolini, and the generals were away at their front tour, the Italian diplomats had remained behind, and again were guests of Foreign Minister von Ribbentrop. During the afternoon of Aug. 26th, they were given a tour of Lotzen, 25 miles southeast of the *Wolfsschanze,* its ancient Boyen fortress, and the military cemetery at Jagershohe, before returning to the *FHQ* in the late afternoon…

"Shortly after the *Führer* and his guests had flown out of Terespol, FG Grundmann and GC Schmidt left in a southerly direction toward *FHQ South.* Arriving at 11:30 AM, Aug. 27th, they joined FG Naehring in Camp Westal. At 3 PM, a tight security watch was established throughout *South* under the watchful eye of 1st Lt. Kurt Thomas, *FHQ Commandant…*

"At 5 PM on the 27th, Hitler and the foreign minister (von Ribbentrop) then boarded a waiting GC, with a FG motorcycle escort, and were transported over a sinuous road, which hugged the north side of the railroad, to *South…*Between 6-7 AM next morning (Aug. 28th), Hitler and his guests left *Anlage Sud/Installation South* in two groups and were driven *south* in FG G-4s with an escort to the airfield at Krosno….

"At 9:50 AM, Hitler's aircraft touched down on Uman's airfield, where he and the *Duce* were greeted by Field Marshal von Rundstedt and (Austrian *Luftwaffe*) Col. Gen. Alexander Löhr, commanding general of 4th Air Fleet. FG Bock—at Uman since Aug. 24th after its long drive from East Prussia—had set up a security perimeter.

"GC Greiderer—which had arrived on Aug. 20th—was also waiting. Hitler and his visitors boarded the latter's G-4s, and—with FG Bock as escort—proceeded to the area south of Uman. After reviewing an Italian division march past, they returned to the airfield at Uman.

"Cordoned off by FG Bock from thousands of German soldiers looking on, they took lunch at tables laid in the open on the tarmac. At 2:15 PM, Hitler, Mussolini, and their entourages re-boarded the aircraft and flew westward to Krosno, where they had all landed by 5:15 PM.

"In another hour, they had been transported in *Führer Column* to South….At 8 PM… the Italian *Special Train* from *South* left for Rome. Hitler was then driven to Strzyzow, where he boarded *Amerika* and reached Gorlitz Station at *Wolfsschanze* at 7:15 PM, Aug. 29th.

"FG Naehring terminated its duties at *South* at 9 PM, Aug 28th, and at 6 AM departed by road for *Wolfsschanze. Westfalen* arrived in Grossgarten at 10:47 PM on the 29th. When FG Bock drove into the *FHQ* at 5 PM, Sept. 2nd after its trek from Uman, and resumed its normal security responsibilities, the last unit involved in the Hitler-Mussolini front tours to Brest, Niedersee, *South*, and Uman in late August 1941 had come home….

"The *FBB* furnished military escort for the *FHQ* and military escorts when Hitler wanted to travel in motor convoy on tours of the front. …The *FBB* was quartered in Restricted Zones 2, 3, and sometimes even outside the *FHQ's* perimeter…

"Hitler continued to use the black Mercedes (770Ks) limousines in Germany, but when he was in the field—even before the war [as we have seen], they were replaced by the company's three-axle, cross-country G-4s.

"During tours of the front beginning in September 1939, two 7.92mm MG 34s—later MG 42s—were mounted on pintles in each of the *FBK's* escort G-4s…Photographs of the *Führer Column* reveal that the *SSBK* component usually rode in the G-4 immediately behind, and to the right of, the *Führer* car, while that carrying the RSD's Criminal Commando was echeloned slightly behind, and to the left of, the latter.

"In the September 1939 photographs, the darker-painted, rear luggage compartment identifies the G-4 then being used by the *Criminal Commando…*They were always driven by *SS* officers or NCOs belonging to the *SSBK.*

"Although the terminology tended to vary slightly, a cavalcade of G-4s transporting Hitler was often called a *Führerkolonne/Leader Column.* When the latter was escorted by a Front Group, the convoy might be known as a *Front Column.* Beginning in 1940, a convoy of G-4s was officially designated a Gray Column, and all GCs were given the *FPN* 41 400.

"In photographs taken as early as June 1940, a tactical insignia marking (stenciled on the left front and rear fenders or rear luggage compartments) of the Gray Column G-4s can be perceived: an animal's head, painted white, enclosed in a white-bordered triangle, base downward, and measuring 15-20 centimeters, top to bottom.

"Sometimes the border is represented by two congruent isosceles triangles joined to form an even larger triangle. The horned animal (kudu? antelope? Impala?) was depicted uniformly on each G-4 of a Gray Column, but it usually differed slightly in appearance among the several GCs. The significance of the animal is unknown. Sometimes, a small, white, Arabic numeral '1' was painted beside the triangle or diamond to identify Hitler's G-4, while '2' was painted on the *FBK's* G-4s."

Unknown—but probably not unsuspected by Hitler's security forces—an assassination attempt on their beloved *Führer* was, indeed, contemplated by the British Section X (German) of the wartime Special Operations Executive in 1944 using either a sniper's rifle (ala John F. Kennedy in Dallas on November 22, 1963), PIAT anti-tank gun, antitank American bazooka, high explosives, or splinter grenades against Hitler's cars.

Stated the 1998 work *Operation Foxley: The British Plan to Kill Hitler*:

"The cars in which Hitler is driven are always of Mercedes make. No photograph is available of the latest armored, six-seater Mercedes-Nurburg type reported to have windscreens of bullet proof glass of 2 inches thick.

"The black Mercedes limousine…is, however, employed in very cold weather, and Hitler is reported to have made considerable use of this type of car in Russia [sic.]

"Number plates are useless in identifying the *Führer's* car, the Nationalstandard [actually the *Führerstandarte*] being the surest means of identification…It is Hitler's practice to sit beside his driver […KEMKA—sic] in the leading car, unless accompanied by an important foreign personage like Mussolini, or the Regent HORTHY, when he sits in the back seat.

"Hitler's car is, however, usually, the second car in the Kolonne when driving from the *Berghof* to *Schloss/Castle Klessheim* sidings."

This is a remarkably accurate report in many respects, and it led the British to want to attempt an attack against Hitler in his car on the *Obersalzberg*—where it might very well have succeeded if done by a determined, professional team bent on accomplishing their mission even at the cost of their own lives, but it never was—so far as is known!

Indeed, Hitler himself once told the late Traudl Humps Junge—as reported in her superb 2004 memoir, *Until the Final Hour: Hitler's Last Secretary*—the following anecdote;

"He had said, 'I've never feared assassination when driving through the crowds in my car—at the worst, I've been afraid that it might knock down a child."

Ironically, the *Führer* believed that he was more at risk from his court photographer, as he also told her:

"Hitler once amused the company at table by describing a drive with Hoffmann in the 1920s.

"'Hoffmann had bought a new car, a Ford, and he insisted that I must try the car out with him. I said, 'No, Hoffmann, I'm not going for a drive with you,' but he kept pestering me, so finally I gave in, and we set out from Schellingstrasse [in Münich]. It was already evening, it had been raining, too, and Hoffmann was tearing around the corners like an idiot, almost ran into the corner of a building, ignored street junctions.

"'Hoffmann,' I said, 'watch out, you're driving like a madman! This is terribly dangerous.' 'No, no my *Führer*, it just seems that way to you because you haven't had a drink! If you'd put back a good glass or so of red wine like me, you wouldn't notice a thing!' At that, I got out, and I never went for a drive with him again!'"

Enter German General Inspector of Motor Vehicles Jakob Werlin, 1886-1965

Just as with trains, construction, and armaments, the *Führer* had a General Inspector of Motor Vehicles: Director Jakob Werlin of Mercedes' Daimler-Benz.

On January 27, 1942—in the very midst of that first disastrous Russian winter of the Eastern Front war—Hitler made the announcement of this most important appointment for his friend Werlin to become Nazi Germany's tsar and major domo of all things automotive.

The *Führer's* decree formally placed Herr Werlin on a similar plane with two men (and later a third) as yet better known to the German public-at-large. The first was Minister of Armaments and War Production Dr. Fritz Todt (1891-1942), his soon-to-be-named successor, Prof. Albert Speer (1905-81), and Dr. Julius Dorpmuller (1869-1945).

The last named had become involved with the Reich Railway Service in 1898, was named its head on June 4, 1926, was appointed Hitler's Reich Transport Minister in 1937, and remained in that post until the end of the Second World War. Had he lived, most likely Dr. Dorpmuller would have been indicted, convicted, and hanged before the International Military Tribunal at Nurnberg as a Major War Criminal, and rightly so, in the author's view.

Jakob Werlin was a car man first and last, and both predated and outlasted the Third Reich as a company executive for Mercedes-Benz and its corporate entity, Daimler-Benz AG (most recently known as Daimler-Chrysler). His is a largely untold story of World War II that shall be rectified here and now.

He was born on May 10, 1886, at Andritz in Steirmark, near Graz, and thus—like his future *Führer*—was an Austrian, and not a German. After having attended a trade school, Werlin began his formal automotive career in 1907 as an intern at the Puch firm in Graz. In 1911, he took over the firm's branch office in the Hungarian capital of Budapest, remaining there until the Great War broke out in 1914.

According to a letter in the Mercedes-Benz archives of June 13, 1939, to a Mr. Gilbert W. Luenefeld in Berlin, Werlin was a "well-known motorcycle racer, [who] enlisted in the military and received a promotion. " In addition, notes the March 3, 1953, issue of *Motor World*:

"As a member of the Bavarian Air and Motor Vehicle Battalion in 1915, he became automobile engineer of the Army Engineer Corps, and in the year 1917 was released to the Hansa-Lloyd Plant. After a short employment in Verel and Bremen, Werlin headed their establishment in Essen."

On November 1, 1921, Werlin was named branch chief at Benz & Cie (Company) at Münich, and after the merger of Daimler and Benz in 1926 as the new firm Mercedes-Benz—the product name—or Daimler-Benz AG, he was promoted Director for all Upper Bavaria, with the home office located in Münich, the birthplace of the Nazi Party. It was here that he met Adolf Hitler.

As I noted in 1999, Werlin joined both the Nazi Party and the *SS* in 1923, the year of the aborted Münich Beer Hall *Putsch* of 8-9 November:

"In 1942 Hitler reminisced, 'I went to the Benz works, and thus made Werlin's acquaintance…I told him I wanted to buy a 16hp. 'You'll decide for yourself in the end,' he said. 'I'd advise you to buy a 10hp to begin with, to get your hand in: it does only 80 km per hour, but it's better to arrive at your destination at 80 than to smash yourself up at 110!' These were so many dagger thrusts at my pride!' Hitler recalled 19 years later. He bought his first Mercedes from Werlin, however."

The *Führer's* future "Deputy for Motor Vehicles" was rumored to have picked up Hitler when he got out of jail on December 24, 1924, an assertion that his surviving children deny, according to author Bernard P. Bellon in his excellent 1990 work, *Mercedes in Peace and War: German Automobile Workers 1903-1945.* According to the letter of June 13, 1939, to Mr. Luenefeld:

"On July 1, 1933, Mr. Werlin became a member of the Managing Board (of Directors) of the Daimler-Benz Company, Stuttgart-Unterturkheim. Mr. Werlin is Advisor of the *Führer* in all matters concerning motor vehicles. We hope to have been of help to you, and greet you with Heil Hitler! Daimler-Benz Company."

According to another statement from its Museum Archive of April 2, 1941:

"Mr. Director Werlin is known to be a trusted confidant of the *Führer*, and was commissioned to answer any questions pertaining to motorization and to inform our *Führer* in any important occurrences in this area.

"In this capacity, he was to tell the *Führer* of many important questions, and (the) positions of business, trade, and industry. Mr. Werlin—except for his employment as head of the Daimler-Benz Company—played an important role in the war in the area of building motor vehicles."

This last sentence was the real key to his power, for as the 1953 article added, "From 1933-45, Jakob Werlin was a member of the Managing Board at the Daimler-Benz Company." Thus, "Hitler's friend for more than two decades"—as I termed him in 1999—was also "Hitler's man within the upper corporate structure of Mercedes-Benz."

His dual role as both a top man at one of Nazi Germany's leading car manufacturers and also as the tsar of the entire automobile industry overall was a unique one for any country before or since—and earned for him a certain amount of enemies from without the orbit of the swastika and the three-pointed star. As I also noted in 1999:

"Just as Werlin was Hitler's insider at Daimler, so, too, was he the firm's link with the highest leaders of Nazi Germany, traveled widely in German-Occupied Europe, and supervised the company's vast Swiss bank account cash reserves, attests Bernard P. Bellon. There, he may have been Edward Schuelte's source for Allied Intelligence's knowledge about the growing Holocaust against the Jews, gypsies, and others."

During the 12 actual years of the Thousand-Year Reich, Hitler made Mercedes the car of the regime, boasting:

"I can claim credit for the things that make the Mercedes cars so beautiful today! In drawings and designs, I tried hard—year after year—to perfect that shape to the utmost…

"According to German author Wulf Schwarzwaller, Daimler-Benz refuses to discuss Hitler's claimed design influence on the Mercedes-Benz cars, and adds, 'No matter what the real story is, Hitler was not only the company's best customer, but he was also its best advertiser.'"

As many leftist authors have been quick to point out, Hitler and the Nazis came to power in Germany with the major backing of most of German Big Business and its aligned financiers and bankers. This included Mercedes and Daimler-Benz AG. Aside from Hitler himself (and later Drs. Speer, Todt, and Dorpmuller), Werlin worked closely throughout the entire period of the regime with the man whom the *Führer* placed in charge of the German economy's first Four Year Plan in 1936: Hermann Göring.

Over the years 1937, 1938, 1939, and 1941, Werlin published under his own name a series of detailed articles on the German automobile industry in Göring's magazine, *The Four Year Plan.*

In 1937, he wrote in *Advancement of Motorization*:

"German motorization under the National Socialists (Nazis) was executed in four main segments. The first started with the *Führer's* speech on ground rules on March 2, 1933. The second was the announcement of the Four Year Plan. At the beginning of the third segment is the groundbreaking for the Volkswagen factory…We stand at the beginning of the fourth segment, announcing the appointment of an authorized agent…to rationalize the building of motor vehicles [the post that took him four more years to attain, so, apparently, there was resistance to his own appointment within the industry itself]."

He also pointed out that—under the Nazis—car manufacturing had risen from a low of 53,483 units in 1932 to a high of 328,267 by 1937, thus out-producing the rival French, who made 183,856 in 1932 and 207,430 cars five years later.

"The German automobile industry can count itself lucky that the *Führer* himself was an enthusiastic and experienced driver," Werlin asserted; well, not really. He had been taught to drive, but never drove himself, preferring instead to be chauffeured by a series of *SS* drivers:

"Six automobile exhibitions have taken place [the German Auto Shows in Berlin] since the power change [of January 30, 1933], and each time the *Führer* gave directional speeches that contained everything of relevance for the motor vehicle industry."

These items included racing, airplane engines, warships, exports, raw materials, parts, tractors, and the domestic labor force.

In 1938, Werlin published the article *Five-Year Motorization in National Socialist Germany: A Look Back and Forward.* He stated of the *Führer* that:

"His interest in the motor vehicle goes back to the beginning of the (Nazi) movement…From that stems the saying of the *Führer*, 'I love the motor vehicle over everything because it opened Germany to me…'

"The automobile export has increased 70% since 1936, an increase showing clearly that the German car is doing well abroad…The password of the future must be: 'All for the *Führer*—all for Germany!'"

In 1939's *Four Year Plan in Motorization*, Werlin noted:

"It was a few years before taking power when the *Führer* said to an intimate circle of co-workers, 'Göring will take over aviation, and I will look after motorization.' What tremendous meaning this simple sentence has won in the four years of the industrial development! Carried by the initiative of the *Führer*, the motor vehicle industry in the reconstruction of Germany took over first place and gave the whole industry an example for direction and pace."

Before 1933, he asserted that:

"The German automobile industry was near a total collapse; it suffered losses it could not bear another six months...The removal of the class war was the first requirement for the development of the industry. At a time when in America 15 of the largest automobile factories hundreds of thousands of employees went on strike and brought the industry to a standstill, Germany can show at the Automobile Exhibit with pride the result of its friendly and peaceful construction results."

"Germany stands today in third place in world automobiles [behind the United States and the United Kingdom]." He also discussed import and export figures, the rate of exchange and domestic consumption, as well as the Hitler-Göring policy of making the Reich independent of raw materials from abroad. One simple expedient during 1938-39 was simply to seize Austria (where the Hermann Göring Steel works was built at Linz) and all of Czechoslovakia (including the Tatra Works that manufactured Czech Tatra cars).

In 1941, in the article entitled *Eight Years Motorization: Eight Years Projection* (which would've taken Nazi Germany to 1947), Werlin wrote:

"In a narrow circle of the German arms industry stand those significant parts of the German industry in the foreground that serve the military on land, in water, and in the air. This sector of the motor vehicle industry—by the speed and force of the German military—made possible their victorious breakthroughs in the east and the west, and our warfare at sea in our modern speed boats and to forge modern and successful assault weapons and, in addition, destructive weapons against England."

Finally, Werlin discussed what his own future duties would be as the *Führer's* General Inspector:

"Whose responsibility is the advancement and consolidation of all necessary measures for production and improvement of the organization...for reaching standardization, as well as a uniformed streamlined target of all service agencies pertaining to German motor vehicles and organizations of State, Party, and Business...The duty of the general agent (Werlin) took on a heightened meaning for everything concerning vehicles due to the outbreak of war...The necessity arose to change the whole industry and mobilize all energy to keep up with the demands made on them by the War Department...."

He also believed that all modes of transportation had been improved, as well as "the construction of a shipping fleet" (merchant marine) and "improved utilization for agricultural purposes," but it was already too late, since the very night before he was killed in February 1942, Dr. Todt told Hitler that the war was lost, and by the fall of 1943, Dr. Speer would agree with his late predecessor.

By summer 1944, Werlin's fellow executives at Daimler-Benz AG also concurred, and stopped producing cars altogether, making postwar plans to make trucks to haul away the debris and rubble from the bombed out Third Reich, and thus construct a new Fourth.

With the end of the regime on May 8, 1945, Jakob Werlin's task was done, and he left the Board of Directors, but was not cast out altogether by his peers at Mercedes, who were—in the main—grateful for all that he had done for the company over the past two decades-plus.

Notes the 1953 *Motor World* article, "After the war, he independently took over as a representative of Daimler-Benz," i.e, he became a salesman back at his home sales territory of Münich. Neither he nor anyone else was charged at Daimler with war crimes by the Allies. Werlin has found his true place in history at last.

******

According to Prof. Speer—writing in his 1981 (and last) book—*Infiltration: How Heinrich Himmler Schemed to Build an SS Industrial Empire*:

"A new material, known as durofol, now had to be 'used on a large scale for the manufacture of a new invention...' At the same time, Himmler ordered the *SS* Command Office 'to build a noninflammable durofol car as quickly as possible.

"'If the experiment succeeds, then we will have solved the iron problem in automobile construction....Please keep me informed of the development of the experiments. If they succeed, we would be extricated to a great degree from the iron shortage for construction. Furthermore, durofol supposedly does not burn.'

"On June 25, 1944, a disillusioned [*SS* Gen. Hans] Jüttner reported that this durofol was 'artificially compressed wood... It would be suitable for smaller parts of the automotive construction, for instance gears, door handles, window frames, and the like.'

"An accompanying report of Office X of this *SS* Command Office explained: 'Basically, a substitute for nonferrous metals and for aluminum. At the moment, only for smaller objects up to around 500 millimeters in the largest dimensions, e.g., door and window trimmings, interior parts of vehicle bodies.'

"The largest parts so far are factory-made fenders. Self-supporting body parts have not yet been manufactured, since models are not produced; they are planned for the future, corresponding to the advanced development in the USA (Ford). A disadvantage will be that the injuries [dents] are not repairable; instead, they require complete replacement of the part involved.'"

The usage of durofol was found not to be practical, i.e.—in Dr. Speer's comment—"Once again, a project of Himmler's had failed."

On July 19, 1943, Hitler paid only his second and last visit to Italy, to see Mussolini at the famous Feltre Conference at the Villa Gagglia, their last such meeting before the Fascist *Duce's* overthrow by his own party and then dismissal from office by the King. As he himself wrote in his 1943 book, *The Fall of Mussolini: His Own Story*:

"The meeting was as cordial as ever…Since the *Führer* had to return to Germany that same afternoon, it would have been better to waste no time.

"Instead of spending three hours going to and from Feltre, the conversation could just as well have been held at the airfield headquarters or at the prefecture of Treviso, but a program had been laid down by protocol, and no human force was strong enough to change it.

"The *Führer* and Mussolini [he is writing here in the rather stilted third person also favored by the American Gen. Douglas MacArthur] and their suites traveled for an hour by train. Then after another hour by (G-4) car, they reached the Villa Gaggia. [During the meeting] a harassed official came into the room. He apologized for interrupting, then went over to Mussolini and said: 'At this very moment, Rome is undergoing a violent air raid.'"

This was the first and only time during the entire war that the Eternal City was ever bombed by either side, and it resulted six days later in the first fall of the *Duce*, "After this, Mussolini and Hitler had a private conversation…during the return trip by car and train."

In January 1945, Hitler's final secretary—Frau Traudl Humps Junge—was carried by G-4 car to his Battle of the Bulge *FHQ Adlerhorst* (*Eagle's Eyrie*) at Ziegenberg, Germany.

According to my own 2007 work *Hitler's Headquarters From Beer Hall to Bunker 1920-45*, "Hitler resided there from Dec. 10 or 11, 1944, until Jan. 15, 1945," going by car to his train for his very last rides in both the G-4 and *Führer Special Brandenburg*.

He then made his last visit anywhere from Berlin to the Eastern Front on Germany's own Oder River on March 11, 1945, on Heroes' Memorial Day, a trip taken in a Volkswagen Beetle.

This was, indeed, a far cry from the mighty Mercedes-Benz G-4s of the Nazi years of victory! It was, perhaps, a good metaphor for the coming *Fourth* Reich's new position after Hitler and Nazism in the postwar world of the Allied victors instead.

A mighty automotive saga thus came to an end, as the 57 manufactured cars suffered various and sundry fates, not all of which are known, even today, more than six full decades after the end of the war. Many of these cars reside in private collections and museums the world over, and some of them can even be seen therein.

In early 2000, the author was permitted to stand where Hitler himself stood in his G-4 on Oct. 1, 1938, as he entered the Czech Sudetenland at the Wildenau frontier crossing. A photograph of that signal event appears on the rear cover of this book.

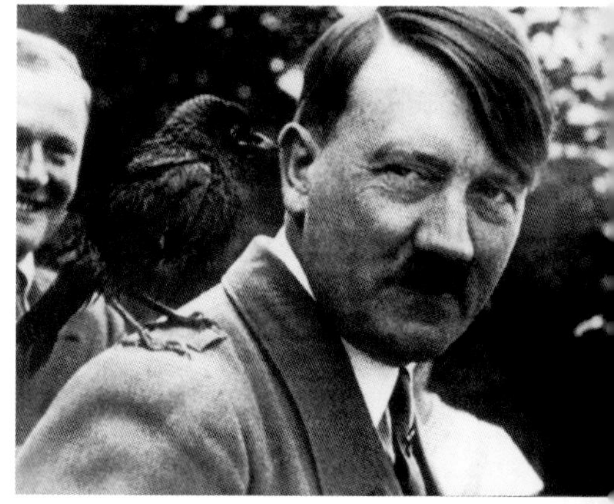

Above: Daimler-Benz Board of Directors member Jakob Werlin (left) grins as a tame jackdaw sits on Hitler's right shoulder at the *Berghof* in 1934, as Rudolf Hess (far right) also looks on in SS uniform. States author Bernard P. Bellon, Werlin "Was always at the *Berghof*, and saw things from the inside." Following his 1942 appointment as tsar of the German motor industry, Werlin was in charge of the Third Reich's "Vast fleet of vehicles—tanks, trucks, and cars—which the military and the German state operated in Occupied Europe." Unfortunately—so far as is known, anyway—Werlin wrote no memoirs after the war. (Photo from the Heinrich Hoffmann Albums, USNA, College Park, MD/USA.)

At the February 1933 Berlin International Automobile Exhibition, Werlin (sixth from left) and Hitler (center) inspect a Mercedes-Benz offering. (HHA)

Right: At a German amusement park before the war—riding in the second car—are Hermann Göring (left) and Jakob Werlin (right) in this previously-unpublished view from the Hermann Göring Albums, Library of Congress, Wash., D.C.

"An interesting view of three modes of German military transportation standing by at Mönichkirchen in Austria in April 1941: *Special Train Amerika*, a line of G-4s with all tops up, and four BMW E 12 motorcycles with sidecars, introduced into the Army in 1935. Note, too, the clear plastic face shields worn by their drivers and sidecar riders," from my 1999 work. (HHA)

"A wide-angle view of Hitler's G-4, top up, parked next to his wartime *Sonderzug* [*Special Train*] codenamed first *Amerika* and later *Brandenburg* (a Mark or Province of Prussia.) Note the car tracks in front of the car, running perpendicular," also from my 1999 work. (HHA)

From my 1999 study, "A close-up of the G-4's right-front side, showing rear-view mirror on the back of the searchlight (including an RSD officer's reflection), spare tire tread, directional signal in rectangular box, and empty pennant staff. The scene is the railway station at Mönichkirchen, a small village in Austria, from which Hitler used *Amerika* to direct his spring 1941 Balkan campaigns against Greece and Yugoslavia." In the distance, glaring at the camera, is *SS* adjutant Gen. Julius Schaub. (HHA)

Duce and *Führer* look over the Ukrainian countryside on Aug. 28, 1941, on Hitler's aircraft. (HHA)

Duce and *Führer* land at Uman Airfield in the German-occupied East, Aug. 28, 1941. (HHA)

At Uman Airfield in the then Soviet Ukraine on Aug. 28, 1941, from left to right: Italian Ambassador to Germany Dino Alfieri, unknown officer, Foreign Office liaison Ambassador Walther Hewel, unidentified officer, German Foreign Minister Joachim von Ribbentrop, Mussolini, German Ambassador to Rome Hans-Georg von Mackensen, two unknown officers, Hitler, Martin Bormann, Field Marshal Gerd von Ribbentrop, a pair of unidentified officers, Col. Gen. Karl Bodenschatz, unknown officer, and Austrian *Luftwaffe* Col. Gen. Alexander Löhr. The *Führer* left Mussolini in the company of Field Marshal von Rundstedt while he mingled with German soldiers there in a friendly, joking fashion, as seen here. The *Duce* was miffed, as Ambassador Alfieri recalled in his excellent postwar memoir, *Dictators Face to Face*: "'Hitler might have taken me with him when he went to speak to the troops, instead of leaving me with old Rundstedt! Did you notice how unsoldierly the *Führer* looked when he was among his men?' the *Duce* asked with a dig at his supposed Axis Pact 'partner.'" (Previously-unpublished photo from the Heinrich Hoffmann Albums, USNA, College Park, MD/USA.)

A German wartime combat art painting of Hitler at the front among his Army and *Luftwaffe* troops. (Painting from U.S. Army Combat Art Collection.)

Lunch at the airfield, from left to right: German Army Col. Gen. Hans-Gunther von Kluge, *Luftwaffe* Field Marshal Albert Kesselring, Mussolini (wearing Royal Italian Army field marshal's uniform), and Hitler. (HHA)

Hitler (right) being greeted by German Army Field Marshal Gerd von Rundstedt, with a G-4 behind them serving as a backdrop. Recalled a German architect born in 1929 in 1973 of an occasion when he saw Hitler, he recalled, "At Rostock railroad station, together with Mussolini. All we did was scream '*Duce! Duce!*' Adolf was in a second car [sic], and *Il Duce* up ahead...It was a sensation, like a Catholic procession, that's what their driving past was like." (HHA)

From my 1999 work: "Thursday, Aug. 28, 1941 at Uman in the Ukraine, in Nazi-occupied former Soviet territory. One of those Fascists who accompanied the *Duce* on his trip to visit Italian units fighting with the Germans in Russia was Italy's Ambassador to Germany Dino Alfieri. He recalled after the war, 'We set off in a procession of (G-4) cars across the Ukrainian steppes.' Here are seen the occupants of Hitler's G-4, from left to right, von Rundstedt [with informal, swagger stick baton], the *Duce* [wearing Italian Army marshal's overcoat and cap], the *Führer,* SS officer Eugen Dollmann, and Kempka driving." (HHA)

Below: At Uman in the-then Soviet Ukraine on Aug. 28, 1941 in a G-4, *SS* driver Erich Kempka is at the wheel, and beside him is *SS* interpreter Eugen Dollmann. The *Duce* stands behind him wearing the cap and overcoat of a field marshal in the Royal Italian Army as Marshal of the Empire, and Hitler is at right, both standing in the car's mid-car jump seat section for once. At rear behind the *Duce* is von Rundstedt, and at right and Italian Royal Army Gen. Luigi Messe. Note, too, the wartime lamp cover on the searchlight at center, and also that all the bullet proof windows are rolled up in enemy territory, a prudent precaution considering Soviet Partisans being behind the lines. Noted Alfieri, "From Ribbentrop's car—which followed a short distance behind Hitler's—I had an excellent view of the *Führer* and Mussolini. They frequently conversed, and every so often, Hitler would stretch out his arm to indicate the direction of his army's victorious advance." (HHA)

From my 1999 work: "Remembers Alfieri, 'Slowly, the long procession of powerful, six-wheeled cars bumped and jolted its way across this boundless, strangely frightening wilderness…As we were a long way behind schedule, Mussolini and Hitler—who had promised to review the *Turin* Division—decided to press on in the hope of meeting the mechanized advanced guard. Very soon, the first lorries came into view, filled with rows of smart-looking soldiers. Mussolini stood up in the car, with Gen. Messe at his side.' Mussolini was disappointed by the overall appearance of his men and their vehicles. Here, the G-4 passes the saluting *Turin* Division troops at left. Note the Fascist standard being dipped in salute at left." (HHA)

From my 1999 work: "Noted Alfieri, 'At Tekucha crossroads, we were met by Gen. (Luigi) Messe, commander of the Italian Expeditionary Force, and Marshal (Ugo) Cavallero.' Here, Hitler leans out of the G-4 to shake hands with Marshal Cavallero. Behind stand the *Duce* and Marshal von Rundstedt, while Col. Dollmann looks on at left. Note also that the bullet proof windows are rolled up in this wartime-hazardous area." Stated the late Italian author Santi Corvaja in his wondrous 2001 account *Hitler and Mussolini: The Secret Meetings*, "Benigno Crispi wrote: 'At noon, we saw a lot of cars coming from Uman. After the command car came the big vehicle with Hitler and Mussolini, followed by other cars carrying marshals and generals: Keitel, Rundstedt, and Cavallero, and followed by the diplomats. Gen. Messe and his staff saluted. The *Führer* and the *Duce* came out of their car and spoke briefly with Messe and invited him to get into their car. Our troops are lined up along the road in perfect order in spite of the narrow pathway.' (HHA)

From my 1999 work: "A good frontal view of the G-4, with its covered license plate and lamp covers. Kempka drives, while *Duce* and *Führer* stand behind the two dictators. Recalls Alfieri, 'The parade of a large detachment of Bersaglieri on motorcycles was scarcely more impressive. Besides being sticky and terribly treacherous, the ground was traversed by deep furrows. Consequently, in order to retain their balance, the riders were compelled to dangle their legs and drag their feet. It was a difficult exercise in acrobatics, brilliantly carried out,' and yet the exercise is not evident from this photo of that described event." Continues Santi Corvaja, "Anfuso described the scene this way: 'I had the impression that the motorization of our units had been somewhat difficult. The troops looked good, and the infantrymen looked like Italian soldiers—not stone- faced—but all smiles and changing expressions. On their faces their joy at having been seen by Mussolini was obvious, since he had ordered all of them over there. The fading names painted on the tanks that reminded the soldiers of home...Gen. Messe looked just like his men: the face of a make-believe tough guy, with sharp eyes....Ribbentrop, who had to accompany me, had a darkly immobile look on his face, as if he was the one being reviewed. I said more than once while he remained silent: 'Beautiful troops!' He nodded from time to time, and when we reached the *Bersaglieri*, he said finally, *'Schone Truppen'* (beautiful troops). Hitler was much more enthusiastic, probably wishing to please Mussolini, who craved Hitler's approval." Dollmann and Kempka are in front, Mussolini and Hitler are in the mid section, with von Rundstedt and Messe behind. Note, too, the spare petrol/gas jerry can in front of the radiator, and also the animal head triangle on the left fender, mentioned in the text. (HHA)

Prior to resuming their battlefield tour of Aug. 28, 1941, in the then-Soviet Ukraine, the Nazis and Fascists pause for a roadside break at Tekucha crossroads. At left are the officers of the RSD backup car and Martin Bormann, while Italian Army Marshal Ugo Cavallero chats with the *Duce* (long overcoat) at center. Von Rundstedt (left) and Hitler have remained in the G-4, their attention claimed by something at left rear, while *SS* driver Erich Kempka leans out of his side of the car. Note, too, the *Duce's* pennant on the right front mudguard. As an aside, one wonders why both Hitler and Mussolini are wearing overcoats in *August*! Were they lined with bullet proof padding for extra protection? Author Alexander Stahlberg thought so in 1943. (Previously-unpublished photo from the Heinrich Hoffmann Albums, USNA, College Park, MD/USA.)

On Aug. 28, 1941 near Uman, two Royal Italian Marshals chat outside Hitler's G-4, with Army Marshal Ugo Cavallero at left, and Marshal of the Empire Benito Mussolini at right. (*Signal* photo, courtesy George Peterson, National Capital Historic sales, Springfield, VA/USA.)

Recalled Italian Ambassador to Berlin Dino Alfieri: "A few miles further on, we ran into the *Turin* Division, which includes the *Tagliamento* Legion of Blackshirts. The soldiers were carefully shaved, their uniforms were in good condition, and their vehicles were spotless. The German officers who accompanied the Italian visitors received an excellent impression. The column had an escort of fighters and was protected by armored cars. The villages seemed almost intact. The people greeted us without enthusiasm. The cars could proceed at only 10 miles an hour because of the mud: it had been raining since five in the morning. Several vehicles got bogged down, and their occupants were forced to seek alternative transport," but *not* the G-4! (HHA)

"At Terespol," with Mussolini and Field Marshal Wilhelm Keitel at center, and Hitler and German Army Field Marshal Hans-Gunther von Kluge at right, the latter carrying his informal, swagger stick baton at a jaunty angle. (HHA)

"Approaching the captured fortress of Brest." Up front are Kempka driving and Dollmann at right, with Hitler and Mussolini sitting on the jump seats at mid-section, and Col. Schmundt in the left rear passenger seat, with von Kluge or Keitel at right. (HHA)

From my 1999 work: "On Aug. 26, 1941, the *Duce* arrives at Reich Marshal Hermann Göring's headquarters in East Prussia. Here, the *Duce* (center) gives the Fascist salute and Göring (left) returns it with his Marshal's baton. Kempka is at the wheel of the G-4, while Hitler is clambering over the mid-car jump seats behind him, and an SS escort officer holds open the door. Standing up in the rear compartment are adjutants Schaub (left) and Schmundt (right.)" Both Göring and Mussolini wear Sam Browne belts over their uniforms. (Hermann Göring Albums, LC, Wash., DC.)

The outdoors airfield luncheon mentioned in the text, but with no tarmac in sight, only grass. From left to right: Hitler, Mussolini, and von Rundstedt, his informal swagger stick baton and gloves beside him. Across the table are Field Marshal Keitel at left and Foreign Minister von Ribbentrop at right, with their suites at the other tables. Note, too, the soldiers watching at the rear. (HHA)

Wearing his white raincoat and with a piece of cotton in his right ear, Hitler (left) shakes during his three-day February 1943 visit to the Nazi-Occupied USSR by German Army Field Marshal Erich von Manstein (center), with the *Führer's* G-4 parked at right. Note, too, the Sevastopol Shield on the Marshal's left arm sleeve, and also the tip of his informal swagger stick baton at the bottom of the frame. In his postwar memoirs—*Bounden Duty*—partly-Jewish German Army officer and von Manstein aide Alexander Stahlberg recalled the following incident of this Front visit, which began on the 17th: "'Tell me, Stahlberg,' von Manstein asked, 'what does *Effendi* really want here? [When Manstein was in a bad mood, he liked to give Hitler this oriental title]' I said…it was not for me to judge…. Toward noon, a long column of cars began to move across the town for the arrival. Saporoszhe had two airfields…The streets were virtually empty. Manstein sat with me in the back of his big, official car with the roof and sides closed. Sgt. Sakolowski was at the wheel. Looking at his driver, the Field Marshal said suddenly: 'Well, Sakolowski, you'll have to come back in one of the other cars. Lt. Stahlberg will drive this car, leaving the other front seat free for the Chief Adjutant, Gen. Schmundt, or Gen. Busse. The *Führer* will sit at the back on my right" (traditionally the place of honor in military and court rituals.) "I looked at the Field Marshal in some astonishment, but he did not react. So I was to drive Hitler! My stomach muscles tightened: me, of all people! What had made the Field Marshal order this seating plan?

Was it considerations of protocol, or did he want to discuss things on the journey from the airfield to headquarters, which, according to security rules, could not be discussed in the presence of a sergeant? On the airfield, the cars were arranged according to rank and station. I sat experimentally at the wheel of the big official car and adjusted the driving seat. After a few minutes, two Focke-Wulf Condors flying nose to tail appeared on the horizon and came in to land. While I was still wondering in which of the two planes Hitler would be traveling, the square standard of the German Head of State" (i.e., the *Führerstandarte*) "was flown from the cockpit of the front plane. Manstein left our group and stood in the airfield a few meters in front of us. I took my place 'back left', as I had seen on newsreels and great State occasions. The pilot of Hitler's plane (Gen. Hans Baur) had recognized the Field Marshal from a distance, and put the machine down so precisely that there was no more than a few steps between the two. The first people to appear were two SS men, who climbed down and posted themselves at its foot. Hitler kept us waiting before appearing in the doorway. The two SS men reached up to support him, so that he should not have to climb down the ladder backwards. This had obviously been rehearsed, and worked extremely well. The Supreme Commander was wearing a dark, leather coat, and Manstein saluted him with his field baton. (In the field, a Field Marshal did not carry the marshal's baton, but a slender ebony baton with a silver head and band.). Only Manstein was allowed to shake hands; all the rest received Hitler's bent-arm salute. For a few minutes, Hitler made no move to walk over to the cars waiting about 30 meters away, but began a conversation with the Field Marshal and his chief of staff, Busse. I kept at a little distance and—thanks to the strong wind—was unfortunately unable to hear a word. Then my eye fell on the second Condor, and I saw a large group of SS men moving towards our column of cars at the double. The cars taken over by SS men disappeared at top speed towards the town—in other words, the delay in our departure had quite obviously been planned. Only an hour later, I heard the reason for this maneuver from Schulze-Buttger, who had stayed at headquarters: the SS men had turned up at the Operations Section building, cleared out the rooms I had arranged for Hitler down to the last piece of furniture, upended every bit of it in the passage and searched it inside and out before replacing it in its original position! After about a quarter of an hour—accompanied by the Field Marshal and the rest of us—Hitler at last walked slowly over to our column of cars, headed by the Field Marshal's car, instantly recognizable by the standard with the gold embroidered crossed marshal's batons on the front right wing. All four doors were open. Sakolowski had already started the engine. Then something unexpected happened: when the four of us, that is, Hitler, Manstein, Busse and I were about to get into the car at the same time, I felt myself being grasped urgently by the left arm and rudely jerked backwards. I turned and looked into the face of an SS officer. All he said was: 'I drive this car!' and the Field Marshal's car was off, without his ADC" (Stahlberg himself.) "I just managed to jump onto another car, also already in motion, which was exclusively occupied by SS guards. On one hand, I was thoroughly relieved to escape the burden of having once been Hitler's chauffeur, but Erich Kempka—it must have been he—had probably not been very well tutored in such matters. The column then moved off at a moderate pace towards the town, where a fresh surprise awaited us when we reached the first houses. In a word: Saporoszhe was on its feet. The population lined the roadsides, and among the Russian men, women, and children I actually saw a good many German soldiers. The news of Hitler's coming must have run like wildfire through the town in the last hour, because when we had driven to the airfield, the streets had been practically empty. Hitler was sitting on the right beside Manstein in the car ahead of me, and even though the plastic side windows had been in place—Sakolowski had always taken care to have good, transparent windows—the occupants were easily recognized. I was able to observe the reactions on either side of the street quite clearly. The Russian civilian population was silent, while the German soldiers saluted with their hands to their caps, which was still the rule at the time, but I also saw some soldiers giving the Nazi salute—contrary to regulations—which meant that they had recognized Hitler. We reached our headquarters without incident, the cars driving round the circle between entrance gate and main building until the first car stopped, before the steps. I was able to catch up with Hitler and Manstein as they entered the house and follow them up the stairs. Manstein gave me a friendly nod, as if to say he was glad I had got through. There were already *SS* men with machine pistols at the foot of the stairs to the top floor. So this was where our dominion now ended. Manstein and I took Hitler to the rooms prepared for him. Behind us, still on the stairs, appeared an *SS* officer with the famous bitch so often photographed with Hitler over the years—a splendid specimen! On entering the rooms intended for Hitler, the bitch was let off the lead and welcomed her master by jumping up and licking his hands. The Field Marshal also had an opportunity to introduce his ADC. Hitler gave me his hand, but this was no handshake, his hand felt like a sponge. He said he already knew me; 11 days earlier, he had perhaps seen me across the map table in his headquarters, but had not spoken to me. I was pretty sure that he would not have remembered me with Papen in January 1933. Then he unbuttoned his leather coat and allowed me to take it from him, and at that point I discovered with a shudder that Hitler had very bad breath. As I took his coat, there was a savage outburst from the Alsatian bitch, and I admit I was not too happy—faced with her bared teeth and her crouching posture, ready to spring—but once again she turned out to be an extremely well-trained animal. 'Down, Blondi, down!' her master shouted, and Blondi obeyed at once. I hung the coat on the clothes' stand, and I could've sworn that in the pockets—just as in January 1933—there were two pistols. At all events, it was extremely heavy. Alternatively, the coat may have had a bulletproof lining. At all events, it was unusually heavy. Manstein and I were then dismissed, to be greeted in the passage—now teeming with officers and *SS* men of all ranks—by the men waiting there: Manstein by Hitler's Chief Adjutant, Gen. Schmundt, and I myself by a very corpulent, grubby-looking man, who had not shaved for days, wearing a gray made-up uniform. He introduced himself to me as Prof. Morell, the *Führer's* personal physician." I have quoted this extraordinary passage at length not only because of how it details a rare example of Hitler being driven in someone *else's* G-4, but also because of the overall aura it portrays surrounding one of Hitler's lightning front tours, and not least due to the fact that I believe that very few modern readers will be familiar with it, just as I was not, originally. (HHA)

The crossed marshal's baton pennant mentioned by Alexander Stahlberg that was mounted on von Manstein's car. (Courtesy George Peterson, National Capital Historic Sales, Springfield, VA/USA.)

Dr. Theodor Morell, Hitler's personal physician, 1936-45, in this previously-unpublished view of 1940. (HHA)

The *Führer* (center) in the midst of a group of field grade *Wehrmacht* officers, just as he is raising his right arm in what most likely was to be his casual, informal, backhanded Nazi salute (often misidentified by writers and editors as a *wave*) at *FHQ* in the East on July 17, 1941. His waiting G-4—with door open—can just be seen at the far right, while at left foreground *Luftwaffe* motion picture photographer the late Walter Frentz captures the scene for the weekly German newsreels. At far left is Col. Nikolaus von Below, and sixth from left is von Ribbentrop's Foreign Office liaison man at *FHQ*, Ambassador Walter Hewel. At the very center at the rear is Jodl, seen just over Hitler's left shoulder in profile is Schaub, with Hitler's *SS* valet Heinz Linge, walking at the extreme right. (HHA)

From my 1999 work: "Japanese Ambassador Gen. Hiroshi Oshima—in the passenger seat with the windows up—arrives to visit Hitler [at *FHQ Wolfsschanze* in 1941], but did not tell him of the planned Japanese assault on Pearl Harbor six months later, the Japanese revenge for Hitler's surprise pact with Russia in 1939 that took the Japanese unawares. Here, through the window can be seen Ribbentrop aide Walther Hewel. Unlike most of the top Nazis, Oshima survived the Tokyo War Crimes Trials, served his prison time, and died in 1978." (HHA)

A formal Hitlerian greeting to Italian First Marshal of the Empire Benito Mussolini (center) with *SS* valet Heinz Linge (right) holding open the G-4's door, all windows up at *FHQ Wolf's Lair*, Aug. 26, 1941. (HHA)

The two dictators seated in the G-4: Mussolini at left and Hitler at right, Aug. 26, 1941, Rastenburg, East Prussia. (HHA)

A wide-angle view of the same scene, showing the white painted on triangle on the left front mudguard mentioned in the text at lower left, and three covered headlamps of varying sizes, in addition to the spare tire mounted in the left well before the door. Note also the covered searchlight mounted just above the spare tire, the rolled up bulletproof windows in the very heart of the *Wolf's Lair* among the saluting soldiers at left, and Col. Schmundt (far right) using the rear wheel foot hole to climb into the car *over* the windows! (HHA)

His Majesty King Boris III of Bulgaria (1894-1943), wearing his Blue Max medal at the throat. (Walter Frentz)

An excellent, wide-angle, panoramic view of Hitler's G-4 on the Rangsdorf airfield tarmac in East Prussia as the vehicle departs for *FHQ Wolf's Lair* during one of the many visits to Nazi Germany of Bulgarian King Boris III, who is seen saluting here from the front passenger seat. All four other passengers are unknown to me, but the man at left is *SS*, while the remaining two officers wear the uniform of the German Foreign Office. The man in the civilian garb is most likely His Majesty's aide. (HHA)

Outside the G-4, His Majesty (fourth from left)—called "the man in the fedora"—chats with Hitler's personal pilot, *SS* Gen. Hans Baur (second from right). (HHA)

Hitler (left) and Mussolini (right) during their July 19, 1943, Feltre, Italy, Axis Pact summit conference. (HHA)

Hitler had the deposed *Duce* rescued in Italy by German airborne commandos from captivity. Here, as they await the freed dictator's arrival at Rangsdorf Airfield near *FHQ Ft. Wolf* on Sept. 18, 1943, the *Führer* (right) shakes hands with the fallen *Duce's* son, Romano Mussolini (1927-2006), as Walter Frentz films the scene for history just over the later jazz musician's shoulder, and a parked G-4 is seen at the far left in this previously-unpublished photograph. (HHA)

Two views of the same event: Mussolini's visit to Hitler at Rangsdorf Airfield on Sept. 18, 1943, after having been freed from Italian Royal Army and police captivity in Savoyard, Italy. In the first photo, from left to right, are von Ribbentrop (long overcoat), Hitler shaking hands with a civilian-clad Mussolini, as the *Führer's* SS/RSD escort officers look on, and Linge standing at the far right. In the second photo, from left to right, Hewel, RSD man, von Ribbentrop, RSD man, Hitler, and Mussolini. In both views, the G-4 with top up forms the backdrop to the scene. Ironically, in their first meeting 10 years before, it was Hitler who had arrived in civilian clothes, and Mussolini in uniform, at Venice in June 1934. (HHA)

Another view of the same scene and event, with Ambassador Hewel (left) in conversation with his chief, von Ribbentrop (right); again, with the gleaming G-4 as an impressive photographic backdrop. The uniforms were personally designed by the German Foreign Minister himself upon taking office in February 1938. (Walter Frentz)

A famous view from my first book for Ulric Publishing, *Apex of Glory: Benz, Daimler and Mercedes-Benz 1885-1955*, in 2006: "*Führer Headquarters* at *Ft. Wolf* in East Prussia. Hitler's G-4 passing the officers' Guard Post 1, turning north to enter Security Circle 1 through the West Gate, Kempka at the wheel. Hitler had a shepherd dog's head painted to the left front mudguard of this G-4. Photograph taken in 1941." Looking at the *top* of the triangle in an earlier photograph in this volume, I have now concluded that the animal was *not* a dog, but perhaps an antelope or urdu, as noted earlier by Dr. Peter Hoffmann. Note, too, that the front license plate is covered, as are all the various size headlamps, and both sun visors are in the up position on the windshield. Dr. Raiber also noted in *After the Battle* in 1979, "No trace of the guard house could be found." (HHA)

The legendary Mercedes-Benz G-4 cross-country touring car and parade *wagen* saga lives on! (King & Country Shop advertisements.)

Bibliography

Books

At Hitler's Side: The Memoirs of Hitler's Luftwaffe Adjutant 1937-45 by Nikolaus von Below, London, Greenhill Books, 2001

The Anschluss by Gordon Brook-Shepherd, Philadelphia, 1963

Apex of Glory: Benz, Daimler and Mercedes-Benz 1885-1955 by Blaine Taylor, Shropshire, England, 2006

Blitzkrieg in the West: Then and Now by Jean Paul Pallud, London, *After the Battle,* 1991

Bounden Duty: The Memoirs of a German Officer 1932-45 by Alexander Stahlberg, London, Brassey's, 1990

Car, London, DK Eyewitness Books, 2005

Crown of Thorns: The Reign of King Boris III of Bulgaria by Stephane Grieff, Lanham, MD, Madison Books, 1987

Dictators Face to Face by Dino Alfieri, New York, New York University Press, 1955

The Fall of Mussolini: His Own Story by Benito Mussolini, New York; Farrar, Strauss and Company, 1948

Fighter General: The Life of Adolf Galland by Col. Raymond F. Toliver and Trevor J. Constable, Zephyr Cove NV, AmPress Publishing, 1990

Führer-Begleit-Battalion Frontgruppen by Richard Raiber, MD; Hockessin, DE/USA, unpublished manuscript

The German Campaign in Poland by Maj. Robert M. Kennedy, Washington, DC, US Government, 1956

Guarding the Führer: Sepp Dietrich, Johann Rattenhuber and the Protection of Adolf Hitler by Blaine Taylor, Missoula, MT, Pictorial Histories Publishing Company, Inc., 1993

Hitler and the Power of Aesthetics by Frederic Spotts, Woodstock, NY, The Overlook Press, 2003

Hitler and Mussolini: The Secret Meetings by Santi Corvaja, New York, Enigma Books, 2001

The Hitler Albums: Mussolini's State Visit to Germany, Sept. 25-29, 1937, by Roger James Bender and David Fasold, Mountain View, CA, R. James Bender Publishing Company, 1970

Hitler's Austria: Popular Sentiment in the Nazi Era, 1938-45 by Evan Burr Bukey, Chapel Hill, NC, The University of North Carolina Press, 2000

Hitler's Headquarters from Beer Hall to Bunker 1920-45 by Blaine Taylor, Dulles, VA, Potomac Books, Inc., 2007

Hitler's Military Headquarters: Organization, Structures, Security, and Personnel by Aaron L. Johnson, San Jose, CA, R. James Bender Publishing Co., 1999

Hitler's Personal Security by Peter Hoffmann, Cambridge, MA, The MIT Press, 1979

Hitler's War by David Irving, New York, The Viking Press, 1977

Hitler Was My Friend by Heinrich Hoffmann, London, Burke, 1955

Infiltration: How Heinrich Himmler Schemed to Build an SS Industrial Empire by Albert Speer, New York, Macmillan Publishing Company, 1981

Inside Hitler's Headquarters by Walther Warlimont, New York; Frederick A. Praeger, Pusblishers, 1964

Mercedes-Benz Parade and Staff Cars of the Third Reich: An Illustrated History by Blaine Taylor, Consohocken, PA, Combined Publishing Company, 1999

Münich: The Price of Peace by Telford Taylor, Garden City, NY, Doubleday & Company, Inc., 1979

Operation Foxley: The British Plan to Kill Hitler, Richmond, UK, Public Record Office, 1998

Poland 1939: The Birth of Blitzkrieg by Stephen J. Zaloga, Oxford, UK, Osprey Publishing Company, 2002

Rommel by Desmond Young, London, Collins, 1950

The Third Reich: Then and Now by Tony Le Tissier, London, After the Battle, 2005

Until the Final Hour: Hitler's Last Secretary by Traudl Junge, New York, Arcade Publishing, Inc., 2002

The Wages of Destruction: The Making and Breaking of the Nazi Economy by Adam Tooze, New York, The Viking Press, 2006

The War Path: Hitler's Germany 1933-39 by David Irving, New York, The Viking Press, 1978

Museums, Archives, Libraries, and Collections

The Daimler-Benz Museum, Stuttgart, Federal Republic of Germany

The Danzig Study Group, Baltimore, MD/USA

The Hermann Göring Albums, The Library of Congress, Washington, DC

The Eva Braun Hitler Albums, The US National Archives, College Park, MD/USA

The Walter Frentz Photographic Collection, Federal Republic of Germany

The Heinrich Hoffmann Albums, The US National Archives, College Park, MD/USA
The Imperial Palace Auto Collection, Las Vegas, NV/USA
The Joachim von Ribbentrop Albums, The US National Archives, College Park, MD/USA
The US Army Signal Corps, the US National Archives, College Park, MD/USA
National Capital Historic Sales, George Petersen, Springfield, VA/USA

Magazine Articles

"Adolf Hitler: The Dictator and His Automobiles," *Automotive News: The Centennial Celebration of the Car,* Blaine Taylor, Oct. 30, 1985
"Danzig: The First Shots of World War II," Wiktor Kurowski, *After the Battle,* 1989
"G-4 Mercedes Staff Cars," *Military Machines International,* Blaine Taylor, March 2005
"Sabres and Tanks," Justin Tonna, *Military Illustrated,* September 2007

Films and Documentaries

Assorted Nazi Political Films 1932-43, International Historic Films
To Be or Not to Be starring Mel Brooks and Anne Bancroft, 1983

Wartime: from left to right: Unknown man, Hitler, unidentified officer, Dr. Ferdinand Porsche, Col. Gen. Alfred Jodl (wearing sun glasses), unknown Army officer, Dr. Albert Speer, and *SS* Gen. Julius Schaub. At the far left, the second *SS* officer from the right is Hitler's servant, Heinz Linge. The scene is a weapons demonstration at FHQ Wolf's Lair. (HHA.)

At a wartime weapons demonstration are seen, left to right, Field Marshal Keitel (third from left), then Hitler, and finally the "Car Czar" Jakob Werlin (civilian suit.). (Previously-unpublished photo, HHA.)

Other Books by Blaine Taylor

Guarding the Fuhrer: Sepp Dietrich, Johann Rattenhuber and the Protection of Adolf Hitler (1993)
Fascist Eagle: Italy's Air Marshal Italo Balbo (1996)
Mercedes-Benz Parade and Staff Cars of the Third Reich (1999)
Volkswagen Military Vehicles of the Third Reich (2004)
Apex of Glory: Benz, Daimler and Mercedes-Benz 1885-1955, Ulric Publishing (2006)
Hitler's Headquarters from Beer Hall to Bunker, 1920-1945 (2007)
Hitler's Engineers: Fritz Todt and Albert Speer/Master Builders of the Third Reich (2009)